R

'After watching my parents endure the pain of divorce, I saw firsthand that it can be one of the most difficult times in a person's life. This guide provides you with the power to survive divorce free from self-sabotaging fear and anger. It will show you how to focus positively on new goals and hopes, support your children, and realise that you have the emotional strength to build a new life. Follow this guide, full of helpful advice and strategies to cope, and you will find your feet on the path to recovery, giving yourself the chance to sail off into your future... a future of happiness.'
Hal Elrod, #1 bestseller author, The Miracle Morning (www.MiracleMorningBook.com)

'This is a powerful book, with plenty of helpful advice, insight and information that will prove priceless if you are navigating divorce. Whatever you're feeling or going through, this book will help you survive the many challenges you face, and come through your experience feeling stronger than you could ever have imagined. I can testify that running has changed who I am. It helped me overcome the odds and get through two divorces. Through running I was able to help change society's perception of women. When we are at our lowest running can be our best friend. Read this book and learn how it can do this for you, too.'
Kathrine Switzer, first woman to officially run the Boston Marathon, founder of the 261 Fearless Empowerment Movement, author of Marathon Woman, and two-time divorce survivor (now happily married for 30 years).

'Every once in a while, we open a book and see ourselves leap off the pages. That's exactly what I experienced when I cracked open The Divorce Survival Guide for the first time. At just 24, I found myself navigating the waters of divorce with not a single person in my life who had shared the experience. No matter where I turned, friends, family, and co-workers just didn't understand. Like Tina Chantrey, I found my solace in running, but if her book had been written six years ago, I would have found a kindred spirit there, too. Her running tips are perfect for someone looking for an outlet for their many (frequently conflicting) emotions, and her story will speak to your heart no matter where you are in your divorce process. Simultaneously vulnerable, friendly, and practical, The Divorce Survival Guide has everything a divorcee needs to get back on their feet - literally and figuratively.'

Danielle Cemprola, columnist for Women's Running (US) magazine, freelance journalist, and blogger at The T-Rex Runner

'In this wonderfully warm-hearted book, Tina Chantrey reveals her journey through a bitter divorce to finding love again - and generously shares all the techniques that helped save her sanity. Running proved to be her primary lifeline, and so she encourages her readers to use it to banish negativity and build self-belief. The Divorce Survival Guide and its practical steps for surviving and eventually thriving after divorce is a beacon of hope for the broken-hearted that will help all those experiencing a relationship break-up get through it with their head held high. Tina's life post-separation is proof that, as the well-known quote goes, 'It's OK to be a glowstick - sometimes we need to break before we shine'.

Lisa Jackson, clinical hypnotherapist and best-selling author of Your Pace or Mine? and Running Made Easy

'As Tina discovered, without a guide, the path of divorce can be a bewildering, lonely trek into the wilderness and thanks to her warm-hearted generosity in sharing her own brave journey, The Divorce Survival Guide was born. In a relationship that is laced with pain, confusion and emptiness it is so easy to lose your own personal power, dignity and self-esteem. You may rationalise away many of your hopes and dreams, only to settle for so many things you did not want. And yet, if you are the one to end a relationship, what does that mean for you? How will you support yourself financially, physically, mentally, and survive the emotional minefield that is divorce? In this gift of a book, Tina can absolutely say: "I have been through this, so can you." Her gentle honesty and practical step-by-step guidance will remind you that there was a time when you knew who you were and knew what you wanted. You believed in yourself and your life was full of hope and optimism and it can be once again. All things become easier when we are not alone.'

Lynda Panter D Hyp MBSCH clinical hypnotherapist and co-director of the Good Mental Health Company

'If only I could have read this book when I was going through my divorce! It's an honest, inspiring guide to surviving and thriving after a divorce.'

Suzy Greaves, editor, Psychologies

'Whether amicable or bitter, getting divorced is a turbulent and emotional time. I come across many women in our online community struggling to come to terms with the grief of their marriage breakdown. Running has become their comfort, sanity and refuge. Tina Chantrey understands this. Running helped her through the sadness and turmoil of her own divorce. Her book The Divorce Survival Guide will fill you with hope, guide you through the pitfalls of divorce and hopefully get you lacing up your trainers...'

Leanne Davies, founder of Run Mummy Run, the largest online women's running community in the UK (www.runmummyrun.co.uk)

'If you are going through an acrimonious divorce, reading this book will likely feel like talking to a close friend. Tina pours out her heart, asks you questions and shares her tried and tested tips. If you choose even just one of them and apply it consistently, it will help you in your journey towards your happy ever after.'

Una Archer, psychologist and founder of
Help Your Child Thrive

'The Divorce Survival Guide is a hand held out in the darkness, a ray of hope in those long sleepless nights. Tina Chantrey shares a belief that there is something greater that will get us through, no matter how our human spirit is tested. This book is honest and heart-warming. Tina is a mentor to guide you through divorce and inspires you to prioritise your self-care on the journey to a brighter life.'

Janet Smith, counsellor at
www.emotionalwellnesscoaching.co.uk

'Let this be your "go to" book of love, inspiration and practical support to get you through the toughest of circumstances. By sharing her deeply personal journey, Tina is equipping the reader with an arsenal of information and a beacon of hope for recovery post divorce. Whether it's running, or another passion, Tina inspires you to heal, reconnect and emerge the best version of yourself. From this point, anything is possible. Even a marathon!'

Caroline Trowbridge, mother, runner, actress,
Reiki Master and author of
I am Me...You, Us and We
www.carolinetrowbridge.com

'As a psychiatric nurse, I too often see the acute side of relationship breakdowns. They say that death, moving house and divorce are three of the most stressful times a person can endure. I concur! Tina's self-help guide not only offers practical advice during such a turbulent time but also a candle-light of hope and happiness. I met Tina at the start of her divorce and can attest to her enduring strength to push through her darkness. Instead of taking Valium, she chose running. From a mental health aspect, exercise to conquer life turbulence is certainly the healthiest path anyone can choose.'

Melanie Charlton,
psychiatric nurse and mum of three

'Divorce is tough and as much as people say they'll help, it's so hard to ask for it. Like Tina, I found happiness in running - it saved me from divorce, bereavement and severe mental health issues and eventually led me to new love and a new career. I am sure this brilliant book and its wise advice will help many people going through a break-up feel better prepared to meet the challenges ahead.'

Vicky Tzanetis, mum of two and founder of
RIOT Squad beginners' running group

'With its many twists and turns, the journey of divorce is often very distressing and the constant worry about one's children can be overwhelming. This practical, reassuring guide provides calm and simple advice alongside a heart-warming story.'

Natalie Wise, divorcee and mum of two

Tina Chantrey's
DIVORCE SURVIVAL GUIDE

How Running Turned my Life Around!

TINA L. CHANTREY

ZAMBEZI PUBLISHING LTD

Published in 2017 by Zambezi Publishing Ltd,
Plymouth, Devon UK
Tel: +44 (0)1752 367 300   Fax: +44 (0)1752 350 453

British Library Cataloguing in Publication Data:
A catalogue record for this book is available
from The British Library

Cover design: Xavier Robleda, cover image: Mike Bell
Content design and typesetting: Jan Budkowski
Editor: Sasha Fenton
Designs and typesetting © 2017 Zambezi |Publishing Ltd
ISBN: 978-1-903065-86-0

Printed in the UK by Lightning Source

About the Author

Tina Chantrey is a mum to three girls, as well as an author, journalist and running coach. Tina is contributing editor of *Women's Running UK* magazine; her freelance career spans over 20 years, during which she has written on all aspects of health, fitness and nutrition for titles like *Zest, Top Santé, Mother and Baby, Pregnancy & Birth and Cosmopolitan.*

In 2016 Tina, blogging as *shewhodaresruns,* won Silver in the Best Blog section of the Running Awards, placing her as second best blogger in the UK.

Just as importantly, Tina is a runner. You can see her on the trails and on the road, as she continues to prove that you can be competitive in your mid-40s (she continues to place in the top 100 women in her age group in the UK over several distances). Tina is also a qualified running coach. She is in contact with women on a national, as well as grassroots level, where she coaches every week in her local community.

Tina was appointed as one of England Athletics Mental Health Ambassadors when the scheme first launched in 2016; they work in their local community to promote the benefits of running to everyone's mental, as well as physical, health. *#runandtalk*

For Lola, Amélie and Sienna, my three warrior daughters,
who already know what it takes to be a strong woman

CONTENTS

FOREWORD

By Olympian, Liz McColgan

I have been an avid runner/jogger all my life, although I was a bit different from the norm as I went on to win global medals for running. My passion for running was not about my medal tally but the benefits I gained through training. I had a very tough upbringing and running gave me an escape mechanism from the day-to-day life I had to endure. I was bullied, poor, from the wrong side of town, and a bit of a loner. Running for me was a saviour. As I ran my confidence grew, as did my self-esteem. Running actually moulded me into a completely different person and little did I know it, would be my saviour again later in my life.

After 22 years of marriage I went through a very public and bitter divorce. If I had not run I would have lost my sanity. From very anxious days that turned into weeks, months then years with what looked like to be never ending conflict, running was my escape, it brought balance into my life and was the only thing that could clear my head on the bad days.

Running became my motivator. It would have been very easy to turn to drink just to make me feel better, but running saved me. It gave me the inner strength to fight my demons.

At last other people can now learn how running can help them through the most stressful of situations, with a clearer view and healthier attitude to come out the other end, stronger, more confident and in a better place.

I hope you gain as much from this book as I have.

Liz McColgan, former Olympic runner, world champion and London Marathon winner.

INTRODUCTION

*'We already have what we need – the opportunity to weave
the tapestry of happiness every day with the needle and
thread of our own mind.'*
SAKYONG MIPHRAM

When I first started on my journey through divorce
in 2010 I only knew one other woman who was
divorced, despite being aware throughout my adult life
of statistics revealing an ever-increasing trend in
divorce numbers. In that year approximately 40 per cent
of marriages in the UK ended in divorce. I became part
of this number. Yet, in a large village I only knew one
other woman in the same position.

Where were all these divorced people? I desperately
needed advice and support from people who
understood the huge emotional turmoil I was
experiencing, underlined by an all-consuming fear of
what may happen to my girls and me. Yet for me, there
was no one in my social circle to steer me through the
endless bureaucratic processes, or advise on which
solicitor to use, whether to try mediation, to suggest I
apply for working family tax credits; no one to give me
tips on how, and what, to tell my children about what
was happening; no one who could look me in the eye
and say: 'I've been through this. So can you.'

As my separation became ever more complicated
one of my married friends suggested I needed a
handbook to survive the whole divorce! This is my gift

to you; if you, like me, have no one to turn to I hope this guide will help you survive and thrive.

I grew up during the 1970s in a reasonably middle-class village on the south coast. Ours was a single parent household as my parents, too, had divorced when I was six. At junior school there were no other parents who were divorced; my brother, sister and I stood apart as children in this respect. It was hardly an accolade – rather I was aware that although some families were poorer than us, we were poor because of divorce. School trips, holidays, even new clothes weren't part of our lives. I can giggle now about how our reality was different, but wearing 'fourths' (including pants!) after my two older cousins, and older sister passed down their clothes wasn't always great for my self-esteem!

As a child and now again as a mother of three children, my life had been transformed beyond recognition due to divorce, and in neither era of my life was there even one close friend who had shared my experience. Despite swearing that I would never put my children through what I had gone through, I was doing exactly that. I was overwhelmed by 'what ifs', and became consumed by my fear of the future. Even though close friends helped me, I couldn't always control my emotions, which drained my energy and caused me to question my ability to keep going, for myself as well as my children. I managed to keep on top of the practicalities of our lives, yet I was plagued with self-doubt and fear. I was running on adrenaline and getting close to running on empty! If you find yourself as part of the ever-increasing divorce statistic, yet remain surprisingly isolated and alone with your fears as I did, this book is for you.

My experience may be far removed from your own, but it's likely that we will have experienced the same fundamental emotions, and there's a good chance that fear, rather than faith, has entered your life. Will my children hate me? How will I pay my bills? How do I communicate now with my parents-in-law? Am I too old to ever find love again? Whatever your background, education, social status or financial position, you've got just as much chance of triggering an emotional 'bomb' as you navigate the divorce minefield. When it goes off you'll get blown off-track, and you may feel as if your energy has exploded into thousands of tiny, inconsequential particles. You may fear you will never feel whole or normal again. But, also like me, you've got just as good a chance of coming through this experience feeling content, with faith in yourself and your future. I'm going to help you keep getting back up, and finding a new way forward.

When I had the courage to tell the one other divorced mum I knew that I too was getting divorced, she told me it would probably take two years for life to feel 'normal' again. I balked at this. A few months later, an acquaintance told me the same thing. Am I am going to do the same to you? The journey through divorce, to coming out on the other side where you can again feel grounded, secure, hopeful, and even happy, is probably going to take at least two years. That's the bad news out of the way.

All divorces have their own complications due to division of assets, children, maintenance… and only when all these issues have been sorted can you begin to let your true emotions settle. Dare I say that it may even take another two years before you feel truly liberated from the experience and are ready to move on. For some people it will be less, for others more, and for others there may never be a time when they feel they have settled into a new way of living. Unfortunately there is no right time frame to complete all the necessary tasks to end a legal relationship, and no right or wrong way to feel during and after. The only definite is that this is your experience, it is unique to you, and only you can understand and control your feelings, and re-navigate your way in the world when you come to re-enter it post divorce.

The good news is that however hard your experience, however many tears you shed, however deep your pain is right now, you can survive these feelings and start believing in yourself again. What you are going to need more than anything are a few good – really good – friends. If you have children, they too will help you survive this period (though expect some choppy waters ahead as you grasp on to each other through this storm).

Just a few very close, strong women propped me up when I didn't believe I had the strength to face what I thought my future might be. I hadn't worked for nearly three years due to the birth of my third daughter, so when I feared homelessness, poverty, destitution, isolation and loneliness, three women stood by me and gave me hope. They assured me that I wouldn't disappear into a life with no hope of happiness or security. They brought unconditional love and support, into our lives when my nine, six and three-year-old daughters and I, needed it most.

These women taught me that the one thing that will help you more than anything is your faith and belief, in yourself. You can survive this experience and learn to love yourself again. It's time to look at the world behind your eyes. By focusing on positive emotions and feelings and letting go of the negative feelings and emotions such as anger, bitterness, resentment and fear, you can stabilise your life ready to sail off into your future.

A survival guide; this implies that if you get this experience wrong, you will not survive. A little extreme maybe, but divorce can be a brutal event in your life. Although it's unlikely divorce will completely finish you off, there's a good chance you will be at a tipping point... and you may feel your feet are precariously placed right up to the edge of an abyss. You may feel for months or even longer, that you are going to fall into this abyss. The most important thing is that you are already hanging on and you will continue to do so. So there's your option: hang on, get through this phase and come out with some sense of self-respect, dignity and love. The other option – sitting in the corner and falling to pieces – well it just isn't an option, especially if you have kids. It's time to believe you have the strength inside of you to survive this.

What is undeniable is that there are people just like you in China, Russia, Canada, and everywhere else in the world, who are going through exactly what you are right now... feeling the same pain, grief, loss, desperation or anxiety about what their future holds. Wherever you live, one thing is certain - you are not alone.

Is any divorce ever easy or painless? Probably not. This book can't take away your pain, or that of those you love. If you are going through divorce, it's likely that you feel as if the world has dropped away from beneath you. You may have lost weight (or gained it), lost friends and lost some of your self-esteem.

The advice offered in this book will help you re-focus on how you would like to emerge from this life event. At the end of each section there are a series of actions, thoughts or beliefs that will help you survive your divorce experience; for many of them you won't even have to raise a finger, leave the house, or spend any money. However, if you accept all of these challenges you may, at some stage, be rushing out the door into a brighter future. Having the grace, and strength, to choose the options in this book, rather than going down the thorny, lonely path trodden by those consumed by anger, will be less costly to your soul, and those of your children if you have any.

For me, running and exercise allowed me to release my grief and remove myself from many very intense situations and feelings. It became like a meditation that turned negative thoughts and emotions into either neutral or positive ones. Does the thought of running leave you with dread? When you think of going for a run do thoughts like 'I can't run', 'I'll make a fool of myself', 'I'll be left behind if I try running with other people' pop into your mind? Did you know that our early female Neanderthal hunter-gather ancestors (think about going backwards along your female line from your grandmother about 10,000 times) had to run between nine - 15 kilometres every day to survive?

Daniel Lieberman, in his book *The Story of the Human Body*, explains that running at least 10 kilometres every day is exactly what our bodies are genetically adapted to do. Don't worry if you've never run before, or if Usain Bolt or Paula Radcliffe aren't distant cousins. The ability to run is in every one of us.

Putting one foot in front of the other is intrinsically linked to your emotional wellness, even from your first year in life. When you started to toddle and endlessly fell over did you give up? Or did you haul yourself back up on to two feet and try again? You've learnt to run before; I know you can do so again. Reigniting that pure feeling of free will, self-determination and autonomy you can just about remember from tearing around your garden and neighbourhood as a young child may help you refocus on positive emotions and energy during these troubled times.

Whatever your background, positive thoughts and actions and some form of gentle exercise now, such as walking, swimming, jogging, Pilates or yoga, may help you realign with your energy and work with it to move into your future positively, and with love. Follow the steps at the end of each chapter and in no time you will be able to look back and see how far you have come. Are you ready? Good luck!

CHAPTER ONE

*'The greatest challenge in life is discovering who you are.
The second greatest is being happy with what you find.'*
UNKNOWN

My Story

February 2016 marked the sixth anniversary of my husband and me separating. In six years I had travelled a hard road from a dark and bleak time in my life, to being able to contemplate a future that included both happiness and security.

Looking back to the second week of February 2010, I had just had a great weekend, taking a trip to the Isle of Wight to do a 10-mile race, where I knocked nearly 12 minutes off my PB! I was on a high! The next day, everything in my life changed forever.

I had been married for nearly 10 years, though throughout this time my marriage had, like all long-term relationships, had its problems.

My husband and I were from different countries and cultures, in fact, we had vastly different personalities and backgrounds. He was from New Zealand, I from England. He had grown up on a farm, and due to living with dyslexia, had never read a book when I met him. I lived in London and my career was writing. We existed on different ends of the vast spectrum of life we all inhabit.

My personality effervesced with energy: I worked as a journalist, went to college at night to study, or was out with friends at the theatre. I also loved filling any spare time with exercise. I literally never stopped, a throw back to my hyperactive childhood years. My husband worked as a mechanic and was more content with staying in watching TV every night. Romantically, and idealistically, I chose to focus on the glamour of him being a Kiwi, and the prospect of living with him in a different country in the future, rather than questioning whether our personalities were truly suited for a long-term relationship.

I knew he preferred the rave culture of London in the 90s, whereas I loved café and bistro evenings spent with friends. He had lived in London for a year before he met me and had never cooked for himself in that time, whereas I had always enjoyed the social event that cooking with flatmates offered. We were physically attracted to each other, and we enjoyed each other's company, but were vastly different in personality and expectations. I didn't give this reality a second thought for years; I chose to look past it. When my husband asked me to move to New Zealand with him I said yes, without even thinking through the implications. When we got to New Zealand and he wasn't happy, we discussed moving to Australia. Our first daughter had been born by then; she was three months old when we moved countries again. I agreed again, without really thinking of how hard it would be to move to another new country with a baby. I was guilty of failing to think through such massive life experiences, and approached each issue with supreme naivety.

In Australia we struggled to get by on one wage, and I felt incredibly isolated with a new baby and no support network. We discussed moving back to England and after two years away we came back. Moving countries three times in two years was tough for both of us, and even back in England, that vast cultural gulf between us remained.

I was now in my home country with my family and friends, and he was sacrificing his home and family for me. It was impossible for us to live in our relationship with both of us completely happy, or without one of us making a massive compromise. Yet as our family grew we both worked so hard to provide our girls with security and love. We just didn't seem to be able to provide it for each other.

Ten years of my life flew by having our three children. As I gradually emerged from the whirlwind of having a third daughter in five years, I started to think about running again. After giving up so much of my life to having children, especially my career and financial independence, I wanted to regain a sense of who I was. Running and writing had always been the two constant threads in my life, even going back to my junior school years. I associated running, and sports, with being in control of my life, feeling happy and working hard, especially coming from a military family. By the time I was 11, I would cycle to my dad's naval base to run with his field gun crew. Even as a child running helped me make sense of life, and feel in control.

I had entered my first marathon in September 2009 and felt so excited to tell my husband; but he just turned around and walked away. He had nothing to say, even though it felt like a massive undertaking for me. It was the first time this had happened between us. I felt shock. I finally realised how separate our lives had become. We were both fully absorbed in getting through our own day-to-day responsibilities; he wasn't happy at the prospect of having to help more with the children while I trained, whereas I knew this was something I had to do. Maybe I was being selfish, taking on such a big project with three children, but I wanted some control over my life. I wanted to do something for me.

On that day I think I knew our marriage was over but I refused to give the thought any energy or space to develop. I just pushed it into a room in my mind, closed the door on it and denied its existence. At first I didn't feel I could tell anyone my deepest worries, either. I kept them buried until Christmas. Don't confide in anyone and nothing will ever happen, right? At Christmas I told a few close friends how I felt, and within two months my marriage was over.

Why was running so fundamental? I have to go back to the point of my conception, when the curious sequencing of encoded biological information on one of my DNA strands (donated by my father) resulted in my carrying an un-identified, un-requested physical asset: the endurance gene. 1971 marked the year I was born, and the year my dad set his marathon Personal Best of 2 hours 30 minutes. Running, it could be said, was in my blood, whether I liked it or not, and whether I chose to tap in to it or ignore it.

There had been a running club in my village all my life but I never joined it. I had been a county-standard athlete at school, but never half as good as my dad, who represented the Navy at various distances as well as being part of a world-record breaking Royal Navy team that ran around the island of Malta.

At 18 I couldn't wait to move away to university then lived in London, New Zealand and Australia before coming back home to live 12 years later. I saw the runners around the streets and once again I thought about joining the club, but instinct this time stopped me. I remember thinking to myself that if I joined the club I may meet someone else - someone more like me.

I believed if I could carry on as I was, bringing up my three girls, immersing all my energy and spirit into them, I could exist in my marriage. If I chose to put myself first, I feared I may discover the old me, which was energetic, determined, outgoing, unwilling to compromise. So I plodded on, not in a bad place but not truly happy. As there was no emotional connection with my husband, there was no one I could talk to about my deepest feelings or my dreams of the future.

After having my third daughter, getting out of the door to do anything for myself, whether social or otherwise, seemed impossible. The first few years of her life whirred by, as if I was caught in the middle of a spinning top that refused to slow down. Once she started pre-school I tried to rediscover a sense of 'me' again. I kept trying to run by myself but I struggled to find any fitness. When a friend said the village running club was holding a beginner's course I signed up.

'The only thing more unthinkable than leaving was staying; the only thing more impossible than staying was leaving. I didn't want to destroy anything or anybody.'
ELIZABETH GILBERT: EAT, PRAY, LOVE

Midlife Crisis

As soon as I joined the running club my running took off and within a few months I ran a half marathon, which was my first since the age of 15. Running improved my self-esteem at a point in time when it had spiralled downwards, and it allowed me to meet people who didn't want to talk about pregnancy, babies or children. Going to races allowed me to escape the routine of my life, as well as the small village I lived in, if only for a few hours.

Yet as my running improved my relationship started to crumble. Despite the fact that my half marathon went through our village, my husband didn't show up or bring our three girls to cheer me on, even though he knew exactly where the route would be. I was devastated. I was upset when I arrived home but he didn't understand why it was so important for me to have him and the children supporting me.

He wasn't a monster or tyrant. He was merely trying to live his life, and worked hard to support the children. We didn't inhabit each other's worlds though, and he definitely didn't seem to grasp how important it was for me to have a life outside of being a mum.

In January, as I sat in our living room looking out at the bleak, grey-soaked skies, I asked myself: 'What would I do if one of my daughters came to me, as a grown woman, with three children of her own, and asked me what she should do if she was in the same situation?'

I couldn't tell one of my girls to stay in a relationship where she was unhappy just so that no one else would get hurt. I hadn't brought them up to undervalue themselves that much. It was my answer: I couldn't stay in my marriage in order to protect my husband or children – I could only stay if I believed we had a future together that was based on love.

In February I told my husband I didn't want to be married to him anymore. For the next few weeks we discussed our relationship endlessly, and I returned over and over to my belief that we had both married the wrong person. Those first two weeks were the most emotionally draining of my life. We couldn't talk until the children went to bed, and then night after night, we went round and round in circles. I dreaded every evening. I would be exhausted from the day and the emotional stress I was under, and then from nine every night we would revisit the same issues. This could go on to midnight and beyond. My husband was in shock because I had told him I no longer wanted to be married to him.

I explained how I had lost any emotional connection to him – how even though I loved him I no longer was in love with him. I knew he was exhausted every day from work, but when I first explained how perfunctory our relationship was, he couldn't understand why I was unhappy, or why it wasn't enough for me. Going to work, and looking after the children, was enough for him, whereas I wanted and needed an outlet that allowed me to have individual goals. My husband never seemed to understand this side of my personality.

I tried to explain that I felt I needed more from a relationship. How my life was filled with looking after the girls but little else. Being a deep, spiritual person I wanted to discuss life, to make sense of it. My husband wasn't spiritual. He believed we lived, died and that was that. There was no scope for discussion – which was fine during the years when looking after babies and children was leaving me catatonic, but when life settled down and my youngest got past babyhood, a deep loneliness settled in beneath my skin.

Then, simple gestures that we all crave just weren't part of our life together. During each pregnancy and birth I had a lot of complications and difficulties, especially with my hips and lower back, but my husband couldn't relate to this, due to his own exhaustion. During our marriage he never cooked for me, there were never any texts sent to let me know if he was going to be late home from work. And I fought for years to get him to make me a cup of tea in the morning, without much success! He worked hard. I looked after the children. If over the years, I bought up my feelings about life's strange twists and turns, or issues that were causing problems, he refused to talk about them, and he withdrew further into himself.

My side was very clear, and painful to admit. I no longer loved my husband.

After those first few weeks of discussion I was due to do a 20-mile race, the final part of my first marathon training. Being so physically and emotionally drained, I gave up hope of participating. But my friend Mel told me I had to do it, so I went and ran 20 miles to the minute of the time I had hoped for. Looking back, I have no idea how I managed to keep going, especially as I was doing this with an unexplained pain in my solar plexus area. But I did.

When I got back home nothing had changed. I couldn't expect my husband to become a different person. Although we functioned well together in sorting out the practical details of daily life in our family, there was no spiritual or emotional connection between us. Deep down I knew that saving our marriage was never going to happen. Even though my husband asked for six months to prove that we had a future, I couldn't agree as now I was convinced that he wasn't the right person for me to spend the rest of my life with. Like so many people approaching my forties, I had slowly, subconsciously, been questioning my life and value systems. My 40th birthday was fast approaching and, whether you call it a mid-life crisis or envisage this stage of life as an interval, with the first half of our lives having coming to a close as we await the second phase to come. Well, I knew I was deeply unhappy.

Looking back, I was guilty of dealing with each crisis in our relationship with an 'it will be okay' mentality. When I tried to raise issues and we failed to talk them through, I let go of them rather than fighting to resolve the problem. Growing up in a divorced household was probably the reason for this. My parents' divorce was as full of as much pain, anger and bitterness as any, and it seemed to us as children that we were never allowed to forget it, so in my immature mind I believed I was somehow partly to blame. Did I have the courage in my own marriage to say this is not working for me? Or were we simply facing issues all young families encounter?

Because of my own childhood experience, I avoided walking away from a relationship and became increasingly unhappy. I clung to it far too long, fearing the consequences of making the break for my children and myself if I gave up. I believed that I could stay in the marriage until the children were older and look at the situation again then. In discussions with friends quite a few shared similar feelings. They weren't really 'in love' with their husbands, but they wouldn't leave because of the way it would impact on their children. I also didn't believe that I could support the children on my own.

Life wasn't a perpetual cycle of doom and gloom. My children were a daily source of insight and despite the exhaustion of having three energetic and strong-minded girls to care for, I felt truly blessed to be their mum. Three children can easily occupy every waking moment of your day, as well as those you spend asleep, but as I approached 40, I became increasingly aware of the gaping chasm in my life. Our daily routine was monotonous - three school-runs plus the daily feeding, cleaning and chivvying of three girls. On top of that, a domestic goddess I was not!

It was the rare, quiet moments when all the domestic chores were done and the children in bed that the truth would come rushing into my head. I could stay in a relationship that made me unhappy for the sake of the children, or I could leave it and cause everyone in the family grief, pain and anger. How could I be responsible for putting my children through what I had experienced? I couldn't: and so overstayed in the relationship.

After two weeks my husband was still trying to convince me there was a future for us, and however hard I tried to get through to him, he never truly listened. I booked us into a session at Relate. That day I feared for my life.

***

Suggestions
This is the one time in your life when you need to call on friends for support and help with your children. Have the courage to ask for help when you need time to yourself, or the space to deal with the changes going on

around you. Struggling on alone, through a dark wave of exhaustion will not help you, or your children, get through such immense change. I guarantee one day you will be able to return the favour.

For practical information about every aspect of divorce, visit **www.gov.uk/divorce**

Try to make contact with other women in your position. Unless you live among several divorced women, and despite generalised statistics that the media throw around, it's probably likely that you won't know any other women who have experienced divorce. Organisations like the Maypole Women (**www.maypole.org.uk**) were set up by women who have experienced separation, divorce and the family court system, and can help you as you go through the process. Search online for a local support group or forum to connect with other women. If there isn't one, could you set up your own?

- Be kind to yourself. This stage is tough. Use affirmations to stay focused and positive. Tell yourself: *'I am strong and will survive this experience'* or *'I believe my future will be full of happiness'*. Create images in your mind of yourself in this future. Avoid negative people and negative self-talk or gossip – this only perpetuates your inner struggle.
- If you can, find time to meditate. Download apps, such as *Stop, Breathe & Think,* or Wayne Dyer's *I Am Wishes Fulfilled Meditation,* which can guide you in mindfulness. This will help you clear your daily thoughts from any negative emotions.
- Turn your eyes inwards: believe in yourself and never under-estimate your inner strength. We create our reality with our thoughts and emotions, so see yourself in control and calm, and focus on feeling these emotions as often as you can.

***

Step One to a New You
Take the first step in realigning your body, and energy, to your new life. Think about starting some gentle exercise – it will give you a feeling of being in control of your life. Try an exercise class at a local gym, go for a walk with a friend, a swim or find a local running club. If this seems overwhelming, ask a friend if they will come, too.

Leisure centres offer an amazing array of fast-moving, engaging and fun classes today.

- Express classes exist for those who have little spare time.
- Fitness and health, such as yoga, Pilates and circuits, unwind and re-energise.
- Bodybalance, yogalates, water workouts, such as aqua gym, aqua jogging, aqua Zumba, along with calorie killers such as body combat, tabata, group cycling.
- For toning and strength, try BootCamp, bodypump or Fit Ball.

Many of these organisations offer crèche facilities as well.

Being outside and exercising in nature has been proven to boost mental health, so for me, running allowed me to clear my head, let go of my emotions and settle myself ready for the daily challenges that I faced.

Turn to the Appendix for my beginner's 10-week training plan!

If this feels too challenging, could you manage one change to improve your daily life? Try swapping your car for your bike and cycle to school with the kids or cycle to the shops or to work or to see friends. You'll reacquaint yourself with the seasons, notice so much more of your surroundings and have more chance to interact with fellow human beings!

Now spend five minutes writing down three new personal goals you would like to achieve in the next six months:

....

....

....

CHAPTER TWO

'A divorce is like an amputation: you survive it, but there's less of you.'
MARGARET ATWOOD

Relate

Complete dread seeped through me the day we went to Relate. I had no idea what would happen during or what would be the result of going, but my instincts warned me it was not going to go well. By the time we left for the appointment I was shaking.

We all know someone or a friend of a friend who has tried Relate, but actually walking in the door, with what felt like a sign on my forehead saying 'I've failed in my marriage and I'm going to wreck this person's life' was horrifying.

Relate is the UK's largest provider of relationship support, and every year it helps over one million people of all ages, backgrounds and sexual orientations to strengthen their relationships. If you think it's an organisation you only turn to when your relationship has broken down, you'd be wrong. Relate is founded on the principle of helping you get the most out of your relationships, rather than just trying to fix broken ones, through promoting healthy relationships in a non-judgmental environment.

Not all people realise that visiting Relate prior to a relationship breakdown is an option; mostly we hear that our friends have attended when their marriage is either in crisis or when it has failed. However, many people who are brave enough to try counselling during difficult times are able to use their Relate sessions to transform their relationship and move forward positively.

Our visit to Relate was my first contact with the vast support network that exists to help people in my situation. This is unbeknown to many who have not travelled the divorce road. Did I go to that session thinking my marriage could be saved? No. But if I had been more honest about my feelings I could have suggested attending some Relate sessions long before our separation. I was guilty of living in a dreamy existence in my marriage. I functioned normally, but avoided looking within to ask about my own sense of happiness, peace and fulfilment. For us Relate meant the agreed ending of our marriage, rather than the beginning of an attempt to fix a relationship that had been broken for years. This doesn't have to be the case for you, because you may be able to use the services of Relate or another support service to re-build your marriage.

The hour or so we spent at Relate was a brutal experience (although there were worse ones to come). I was terrified. I felt as though I was a tiny spider waiting for a giant to come along and squash me.

There wasn't a specific event or outcome of which I was fearful. Never being the type of person to encourage discord or conflict in my life, the thought of having to react and respond to someone's anger - which I had been responsible for - felt frightening. I'm not sure I had really felt raw fear before this. As an adult, I had long since slid into the persona of peacekeeper, and being an introverted-extrovert. I relied on compromise rather than contradiction to keep the peace.

I was afraid of the way my husband would react, yet I also felt a sense of suppressed hilarity about what I was doing, which was going to speak with a stranger about the failure of my marriage. The words 'how has my life come to this?' ran through my mind over and over.

'Names please,' we were asked at reception when we arrived. The building housing Relate looked run down.

'Please sit in the waiting room,' said the receptionist.

I awkwardly sat next to my husband. Paint was peeling off the walls and a sense of doom charged the air. We sat in silence.

We were called through to our counsellor.

'Please can you state why you're here,' she asked.

'My wife has told me she no longer wants to be married,' offered up my husband. 'I want to try and save the marriage.'

The counsellor listened mindfully as my husband explained our situation. She then turned to me. Bile rose in my throat. It was my turn to state my expectations.

'I want my husband to accept that I don't love him anymore,' I replied. My sense of embarrassment left a blush on my cheeks. My voice wavered with emotion.

The words left me and hung heavy in the air. Sharing them in front of a stranger, in a bare and sterile room, I felt disgusted with myself. Guilt, betrayal, abandonment, failure, sadness and confusion were all entwined into the delivery of that short sentence. Why did I feel this way? Why couldn't I say something like 'okay, let's give it another go'? I was driving a stake through the heart of the person I had chosen to marry and to be the father of my children. When you get married you never imagine yourself saying those awful words. Our lives were changing forever.

'I've been trying to talk to my husband for weeks to make him realise this. Whatever I say he doesn't really listen,' I added. My head remained down. I couldn't look at my husband.

'We've discussed our problems and I want time to try and change our situation,' my husband said.

'Are you willing to do this?' the counsellor asked me.

'If I still loved my husband it would be worth trying, but I don't,' I said.

'Would you consider trying?' asked the counsellor.

'I don't want to stay with him for the rest of my life,' I replied, 'as I don't love him.'

I hated myself each time I had to say it, but the counsellor went back and forth between us so that we were both completely sure of what we wanted to say, and do.

We didn't discuss our relationship in any great detail after this. Rather the counsellor tried to help us both state as clearly as we could how we felt, and try and decide what the best solution was at that stage.

'What's the point in carrying on?' my husband started to say. 'She's made it clear how she feels, hasn't she? I thought there was a chance we could sort this out, but if that's how she feels there's no point talking any more.'

I continued to look down. Every word I said was hurting him. Over and over he had to listen to me saying I didn't love him. Our session then ended quite abruptly as he decided it was time to leave. It seemed that he had finally accepted what I had been trying to tell him for weeks.

'What's going to happen?' I asked, as we walked back to the car.

'Don't talk to me,' was fired back. 'I hate you.'

Our car screeched out the car park so fast I thought we were going to hit the wall opposite. Every mile of the drive back home drove fear into me, until it became a pulse in every cell in my body. The car slammed to abrupt halts at each set of traffic lights. On the motorway we drove far too fast. The car became a moving last-chance saloon. At every bend or turn I thought we were going to crash, and I had to hold on to the dashboard to brace myself. We didn't talk, argue or shout at each other. He was far too angry and I was far too scared.

'You'd better leave when we get back,' my husband barked at me as we approached home.

I was under no illusions that I would be unsafe around him. His anger seethed from him. I completely understood this, too. Over a few miles of motorway the love he had been fighting for had morphed into hate.

I could see it, feel it, and sense it energising between us. I couldn't blame him. I panicked in my mind and kept thinking that it had all been my fault. It would take at least two years before life and my emotions, settled enough to be able to take a side-step and not feel compelled to accept total blame and responsibility for the breakdown of the relationship. Getting to that state was a long way off though.

'We need to talk about what we're going to do,' I said when we got into the house.

'If you think you're getting anything from me you're wrong. I don't want to talk to you,' he said walking away, ending the conversation.

I took five minutes to pack a bag before going to find my girls at a friend's house; somehow I tried to carry on as normal for the rest of that weekend as the girls still didn't know what was happening. Every ounce of energy was drawn on to get through those days so I focused on carrying on their routines, while fear continued to pulsate through me. I still had no idea at this stage what was going to happen to us. After two nights away we had to go home. Hiding in someone else's house couldn't last.

We returned and everything was different. Overnight, in my husband's eyes, I became a liar, a thief and a deceiver. When I tried to talk to him on return he blamed me for everything that had gone wrong between us, then refused to talk to me again – he said he wanted nothing to do with me.

Life then changed very dramatically as our marriage officially ended and grief took over our lives. The next week my husband took actions to deny me any access to his money – without telling me. When I tried to buy our groceries, I found out the credit card had been stopped. I confronted him and he told me he had sought legal advice and been told to stop all the access that I had to his finances. The fact the children had no food to eat didn't bother him. We had a massive argument about this – the children needed to eat. He refused to pay – we started to go round in circles as we discussed what was going to happen. My husband's arguments were always the same: I was leaving him therefore I had broken up the family and I would have to 'pay' for this. After I told my husband at Relate that I didn't love him, and he accepted I didn't want to be with him any more his response became one-dimensional - he was going to punish me financially for my decision.

He told me he wanted to fly back to New Zealand to see his family and asked for our meagre savings to be moved into his account. Full of guilt I agreed, without questioning his motives.

He did not travel back to New Zealand.

'If you think you are getting this house, you're wrong,' he told me when I confronted him about our living arrangements. 'You can forget any deluded thoughts you have of keeping the house. I want my money back.' This was his answer when I tried to discuss where the girls and I were going to live. I tried to discuss our options but he 'told' me he wasn't going to support the girls. 'You'll never get any money from me for them,' he said. 'You've broken the family up, not me. You can be responsible for them. I hope you all end up in a council house, living with druggies and losers.'

With no access to my husband's wage the three girls and I had £188 per month (their child benefit) to live on, supplemented by the odd feature that I wrote. Over just a few days I went into brain shock, followed by body shock.

Our house was put on the market. I couldn't see any other option as I visited a financial advisor who told me that, as a part-time journalist, I had no chance of taking on the mortgage. I didn't want to fight my husband for the house, as I didn't want to alienate him from the children. Before we had married we discussed what we would do if, at some stage in our lives, we divorced. I didn't want to repeat my own childhood experience. We had discussed thoroughly how we would always put the children first. Very quickly it was becoming evident this wasn't going to happen.

I was in a weak position. After my third daughter was born I had three years off work. Moving house and having three children aged five and under was tough. Having the children completely changed me – life was about them rather than me. As my youngest had approached pre-school age I started thinking about working, but didn't know if I would be a journalist again. An old friend, Marie, also a journalist and editor, knew writing was a big part of my persona. Marie encouraged me to write for her and suddenly, at the same time I joined my running club, I began to write again.

The night of our Relate appointment also saw me leave our marital bed forever, and it is one of my most potent and saddest memories of my life. I was looking after the children, our house was being sold and with my youngest not yet at school, I was only working a little. I was beginning to fear how I would be able to support the girls on my own.

Grief and fear took over me, yet there were hidden blessings in my daily life. I moved into my middle daughter's bedroom and for a few months, it became an emotional sanctuary. During the next few months and the years that followed, it came home to me that my children truly loved me. It seems bizarre for an adult of 40 years of age to be able to say that she finally knew what it felt like to be loved – unconditionally.

Mediation

Practicalities loomed, and as my husband took action to deny me access to any money, I knew I needed advice on what steps I should be taking. I visited my local Citizen's Advice Centre, in our town library. There I was advised to seek assistance from a solicitor. I visited two solicitors and appointed the one I felt most relaxed with, and she recommended my husband and I attend mediation.

Mediation is an effective, flexible way of resolving disputes without the need to go to court. It involves an independent third party - a mediator - who helps both sides come to an agreement. The role of the mediator is to help both parties reach a solution to their problem and to arrive at an outcome that both are happy to accept. Mediators avoid taking sides, making judgements or giving guidance. They are simply responsible for developing effective communications and building consensus between the parties. The focus of a mediation meeting is to reach a common sense settlement agreeable to both parties in a case.

Mediation is a voluntary process and will only take place if both parties agree. It is a confidential process where the terms of discussion are not disclosed to any party outside the mediation hearing. If parties are unable to reach agreement, they can still go to court. Details about what went on at the mediation will not be disclosed or used at a court hearing. Both parties share the cost of mediation, which will depend on the value and complexity of the claim.

My husband appointed his own solicitor, and I set about trying to find a mediator. Organising seeing a solicitor and a mediator takes time. As I tried my best to look after the children I also became solely responsible for setting in motion the bureaucratic cogs that would eventually lead to the dissolution of our marriage. My husband, being the party who was being 'left' provided no help or assistance in sorting out any official matters. Tragically, he felt he couldn't live in the same house as the girls and carry on communicating with them, so for nearly six months he lived with them but wouldn't talk to them, apart from saying hello or goodbye. My heart broke.

If our Relate session was horrible, mediation, with its endless wrangling and the constant personal digs against me, took me down into a dark, dark place. By the time we arrived, we were acting like strangers. It wasn't an easy experience for either of us. Mediators, holding the hands and guiding people through such a life-wrenching experience are angels on this earth.

Our mediator provided us both with support and resources. Unaware about my entitlement to any financial support, the mediator pointed me in the direction of Children's and Working Family Tax Credits. I learned that I was eligible for some financial assistance and more importantly, this was backdated to the day when my husband and I had agreed to separate, which had occurred directly after our Relate session, several months before. This was absolutely vital. Immediately upon separation I had started searching for work, and was fortunate to find that some jobs started to come in. I almost instantly started working enough hours and earning enough to believe I could support the girls.

The mediator also suggested we read an essential guide to life and relationships – a book that children should be presented with upon leaving school to help navigate them through their adult relationships. The book is *Men are from Mars and Women are from Venus* (£8.99, Harper Thorsons) and remains a best-seller – if you haven't read it, order it today.

Mediation may help you both resolve your separation, both financially and emotionally, without involving solicitors. This is the aim. For me, it wasn't this straightforward, and maybe, by making you aware of my experience, you will be better armed than I was. I naively thought my husband would also attend in order to work out how to split our shared resources, have access to the children, and then go forth into our own lives. I was wrong.

For us, when it came to the simplest of issues, such as sharing the car or repaying the car loan, I had to fight not to be left with sole responsibility.

During the first session we were advised that we would both need to provide full financial statements, so we could then agree on how to divide our assets and provide for our children. We went through our finances – our mortgage, debts, loans etc. The mediator tried to steer us to agreeing an acceptable division of the basic assets. As our house was being sold, the way in which we were to divide any profit became an important area to settle.

Our discussions ranged over house bills, the mortgage, car loan, the girls' savings accounts, and with every point that came up for discussion, my husband restated the same sentence: 'You broke up the family, so why should I pay for anything?'

'If your wife is looking after the children and with one still under school age, she won't be able to earn enough to pay all the bills at the moment,' the mediator advised.

'I don't care – it's her decision, she should be paying half of the mortgage and bills now.'

Whatever either of us said, my husband was adamant: I was to blame, I had to pay. He said, 'If you end up with nothing and have nowhere to live it's your fault, this is your choice,' again and again for two hours. 'I'm never going to give you maintenance.'

During each session both I and the mediator, came up against my husband's belief that as I was leaving the marriage, I was responsible for sorting out all the financial details. At that time he couldn't consider an amicable way of sorting out our joint finances. As the mediator tried to establish a fair division of assets my husband dug in his heels and refused to share responsibility or provide the financial information we needed to progress.

Instead of working out how best to sort out the dissolution of our marriage, he used the mediation sessions to verbally attack me. On every point, if my husband didn't get what he wanted, he would refuse to cooperate or to find an agreement. Then he would become increasingly angry and return to everything being my fault. We attended six sessions, and the mediator tried to sort through division of assets. However, even after this time, my husband refused to provide all the financial information we needed. As each session went on I wanted the whole process to end so I started to agree to what he wanted, just so each session, and the process, would be over.

Maintenance for the children was a crucial part of mediation - yet it wasn't sorted out. I brought up his statements to me that he would never give financial support to the girls. As my husband eventually agreed to pay the bills until the house was sold, we decided we wouldn't have to look at the issue of maintenance until after this happened. Then, we all agreed, we could try and sort it out between ourselves. Even though my husband was angry at me, I hoped, when it came to sorting out maintenance, he would want to help support his three girls.

Mediation was a difficult experience, full of wrangling and arguing. After the first session I drove home, and about five minutes from the house pulled over in the car to ring my friend Caroline. I wailed with primeval grief. It took half an hour to stop sobbing and collect myself enough to be able to go on and pick up the girls. Caroline just listened to my grief, disbelief and pain until I eventually regained control over my emotions. I couldn't hide my tears from the children that day, but I didn't want them to know their dad was walking away from any responsibility for them. They still were unaware we were separating.

As separation progressed into divorce I responded like a four handed tennis player – whatever was thrown at me I batted back, whether it was the right thing to do or not. Carrying on, regardless of exhaustion and anxiety in order to ensure the children's life was not destroyed was my only goal. Caffeine fuelled the desperately long days. For months I was unable to bring any focus on myself, or on my own emotional, physical and spiritual health.

My friends kept reassuring me that we would be okay, and that constant hand-holding propped me up. I could be crying on the school playground but there was always someone to turn to, someone there to whom I could talk. By now I was well into what is comically known as the 'divorce diet'. My stress levels were high, and I was so anxious I couldn't sleep. I felt as though I was trying to thread myself through the eye of a needle.

My friend Mel created a spreadsheet for me with all my possible outgoings and incomings, just to show me that I was going to be able to support the children. We sat together and worked through the financial implications of living on my wage – we worked out exactly what I would need to earn.

Self-help books were a salvation. With no one to talk to about the divorce, books gave me the power to find my way through the lows. Well aware of the universal law of attraction, I didn't need anyone to tell me if I carried on fuelled by fear, my life would disintegrate. I had read books like *The Secret, Ruling Your World, The Power of Now,* and *Learning to Love Yourself,* and I knew that the more negative emotions that became stuck in my mind, the more of this type of energy I would bring into my life. I began to retreat to bed as early as I could and read, reminding myself that the power to survive the experience which I was living would only come from within. As Wayne Dyer said, I knew I had to: 'Be open to everything and attached to nothing.'

My running took a drastic downturn as I didn't have the energy to get to my club training sessions - but it didn't stop. I stopped entering races because there were so many distractions to pull me away from my sport. As my self-esteem was knocked out of me, the miles I travelled on the roads dropped, and the time it took me to complete them got longer. Anyone who has run for a significant period of their lives knows that their running becomes a metaphor for how they feel. Unsurprisingly, my weight dropped. I took on sole responsibility for the children, and my focus switched to handling our separation, so running didn't just go on the back-burner; it got thrown out with the potato peelings. I didn't know if I would ever want to be a competitive runner again. But I still built my runs into my week, and they became crucial in helping me release stress.

I began to find a little time every day to focus on bringing enough work into my life to support the girls. When we were out at the park or on the school runs, I would repeat my affirmations, and the more I did it, the more I began to feel the truth of the words. I still have the sheet of paper on which I wrote them. It was my list of wishes that I sent out to the universe, including gratitude for being healthy, to be able to transform my mistakes into blessings and for being the person in the mirror. I also focused on earning enough income for us. It wouldn't take long before I would get a reply back.

Your life is a complex and beautiful tapestry. As you weave its pattern you are able to create love, peacefulness, health and prosperity. You can also create a life filled with anger, conflict, illness and depravity –

physical and emotional. Many New Age thinkers believe we all have the ability to create our own wish-lists of all that we desire for our lives, and by living as if those wishes are already fulfilled, we can bring them into our reality. This assumes that the feelings that we focus on grow into our reality. It's almost as if putting ourselves into a positive mental state allows us to heal negative emotions, and welcomes the energy into our lives that we need to fulfil our greater purpose.

When you are plunged into difficult experiences it can be much easier to focus on the negative emotions that are a natural response to 'fight or flight' situations, where we feel under threat. In the face of aggression, attack and conflict most people naturally adopt a protective mechanism where they respond to perceived attacks on themselves with similar responses. If your divorce is troubled, it's probably natural you will respond initially with similar feelings, dominated by fear – leading to an almost unconscious reaction of anger. Choosing to change the way you feel and respond to perceived threats isn't always easy, but it is possible.

My initial response to events as they unfolded was predominantly bewilderment. I couldn't understand how our relationship deteriorated so rapidly, and why our children's emotional welfare wasn't the priority for both parents. When other people felt angry about the situation they would be surprised that I wasn't feeling the same, or that I wasn't fighting back. But it wasn't my way. I couldn't expend energy on directing anger at my husband, but I could focus on what I thought the future for the girls and I could be.

Grief took root, in body and soul. She was not alone though, as anxiety and guilt accompanied her. Quite a vast collection of negative feelings had been slowly accumulating inside me. I had made the decision to allow them to prosper, and had become emotionally toxic. As a child I had not been encouraged to freely express authentic emotional responses in difficult situations, because growing up the 1970s, I was influenced by my parents. Their generation, and the one that came before them, had deferred to a pattern of suppressing difficult emotions. If you were unhappy about something at home, saying something about this brought consequences that no woman could survive. Fear again. It planted its seeds very early in my life.

My parents loved us, but I can't remember them providing an atmosphere that promoted the development of our self-worth. They were suffering their own pain as they navigated their own divorce, while being pressured by both of their families to stay together. What young child can frame the words to talk to their parents about their own anxiety, grief or pain? A child's world is a selfish one. A child can only focus on its own pain. I suffered from deep feelings of loss and inadequacy as a child, and continued to do so as a teenager and young adult, but I was unable to share this.

Many people, who grow up in troubled homes adopt this denial lifestyle, where you deny your feelings and your truth. This becomes your emotional history. Whether it is a consequence of living in a household overshadowed by addiction, dependency or loss, the end results are often the same... low feelings and a lack of self-worth. Experts tell us common statements of a distorted reality are 'Things aren't that bad,' and 'I'll be all right if only...' These had been two of my internal responses to most of the issues that had arisen within our marriage.

When I could no longer avoid conflict, the fear that still extended forward from my early childhood, flooded back into me. It overtook me. Just as I had been fearful of standing up to my mum as a child, I was fearful of doing the same to my husband. What was behind this fear? Probably anger. Firstly, a naïve childish anger that life didn't unfold the way I wanted it to, then a subtler, unconscious and selfish anger that my husband hadn't been everything I needed him to be. I still hadn't completely grasped that only I could provide everything in life that I needed for my own happiness.

Being able to express anger is completely natural and essential to one's mental well-being. I could never tell the people who counted that I was angry – about anything! It is still something I find almost impossible, in case it will make me unlovable. My role-modelling consisted of two parents who were both twins. Both sets of twins had fallen out with their sibling, and neither of my parents talked to their twins for at least the last thirty years of their lives. This example made me believe that telling my loved ones the truth about how I felt would inevitably lead to dire consequences and complete ostracising from their lives.

Maybe the issue goes deeper than being a product of a troubled upbringing. Being a female, a wife and a mother also leads many of us to respond by making the most of difficult situations rather than challenging them. I had a rebound reaction to difficulties: I got through them, whether I wanted to or not, believing that things would get better. It was an entrenched belief, and it was one I know my grandmother would have been proud of. That's what women do.

Suggestions

To find out what your options are at this stage, contact Citizen's Advice **(www.citizensadvice.org.uk).** You will receive free, independent, confidential and impartial advice either online, by phone or in person at a local Citizens Advice centre. They can help you resolve worries about benefits, work, debt and money, as well as where to seek legal advice.

- The Law Society has a directory of solicitors which is called 'Find a Solicitor'. This enables people to find local solicitors who specialise in specific practice and who hold Law Society accreditations. The free online website is: **http://solicitors.lawsociety.org.uk**

- If you and your partner can attend Relate **(www.relate.org.uk)** you may be able to resolve the conflict between you or redefine your relationship. Relationship counselling will aim to help you both move forward in your lives with more confidence and less anxiety.

- Make a list of your negative feelings – be as comprehensive as you can. Don't apportion blame to them, just acknowledge them. Knowing them can allow you to accept them and let them go, freeing you to allow higher, more positive and more creative energy and feelings to replace them. Others can't make you negative as only your response to them allows negativity in to your life. Download affirmations on to your iPod (if you can afford to own one) and listen to them while walking to school or doing chores. I put Ester and Jerry Hicks' *Getting into the Vortex* guided meditations onto my phone. Each one is only 15 minutes long, which is just right for the walk to school.

If you are wealthy enough to own and drive a car, never ever listen to meditations and so forth while driving, as the trance-like effect of these can cause you to lose focus on what you are doing and to have an accident.

- Try not to be judge and jury to anyone in your life at the moment. Through forgiveness you can stop carrying around anger, promoting inner healing. It is the greatest gift you will ever give to yourself.

- Can you recognise signs of grief, such as denial, anger or depression? Are these linked to deeper feelings that have been suppressed? Face your fears by looking at these deeper feelings. Can you find ways to express them in a healthy way, without revenge or spite? If you feel overwhelmed by negative feelings visit your GP to discuss help going forward.

- Could mediation be an option for you? Mediation can be quicker, less stressful and cheaper than going to court. Once a settlement has been reached, a mediation agreement can be drawn up. Parties tend to keep to the mediation agreement because they have prepared the terms themselves. Visit **www.civicmediation.org** to find a local mediation provider.
- Do you have children? If so, can both parents agree to try and consider your children's feelings, as well as your own, at this time, despite the pain or anger you may both be experiencing? Even if you haven't told them what is going on, they know there are problems. Avoid indulging in personal attacks in front of your children as these will benefit no one. Don't encourage your children to take sides. There are many organisations that can help you and your children to survive this experience with positive rather than negative emotions and memories, such as:

www.gingerbread.org.uk, www.youngminds.org.uk, and **www.nfm.org.uk**

- You may be eligible for some kind of Tax Credit, so go online and look up the many sites that offer tax credit calculators.
- Contain your financial fears by creating your own financial plan. Set up a spreadsheet on paper or on a computer that shows all of your outgoings and incomings so you can work out what you need to earn. Ask friends if they can help or look online. Organisations like the Money Advice Service (**www.moneyadviceservice.org.uk**) provide free and impartial advice.

Step Two to a New You

If you've managed to start exercising, well done! Walking every day, swimming or cycling every week and running regularly may empower you, by providing you with an essential sense of achievement. My motto, which I've always told my three girls, is 'a strong woman is a powerful woman'.

- If you have started running, aim to run at least twice a week. A walk-run strategy will ease you into exercise. Run to a lamppost then walk to the next, and repeat this as many times as you are able, then walk home. Each time you go out for a run, add on a few more lampposts. Soon you will be able to run more than you walk, and before you know it you will have run round the block.

**Turn to the Appendix to find my
ten-week beginner's training plan.**

- If you need more support, RunTogether (**www.runtogether.co.uk**), which is the official England Athletics recreational running project, will help you find a group or club that is right for you. Don't rush to join the closest club; find a club that has a beginner's course if that's what you need, and find one that offers different intensity sessions to cater for all abilities (at a time that works for you) as well as social events. It's likely that once you join you will stay with your group, so you want to ensure yours will be a long-term relationship!
- If this feels too challenging, then why don't you take yourself down to your local parkrun, (**www.parkrun.org.uk**) and walk the distance. These are free 5K (three mile), family-friendly and welcoming events held throughout the UK at 9 a.m. on Saturday mornings. Kids can also take part, so

you can all get back to nature and have time-out to chat about your week.

Spend five minutes writing down three affirmations for your future here, such as: 'I am earning more than enough to support my children,' or 'I am lovable'.

....

....

....

CHAPTER THREE

*'Holding on to anger is like grasping a hot coal with the
intent of throwing it at someone else; you are the one
getting burned.'*
GAUTAMA BUDDHA (563-483 BC)

Telling the Children

Next I had to tell the girls, or more specifically the
older two, who were old enough to realise that
something was terribly wrong. Having experienced
divorce at a very young age, the thought of causing so
much disruption, upheaval and uncertainty in their lives
was terrifying. I knew I couldn't protect them from pain
but I could support them. The Easter holidays were
approaching and knowing that our house would be put
up for sale very soon, I tried to talk to my husband about
a plan for us to tell the girls at the beginning of the
holidays. This would give them two weeks to digest the
information, and for us to respond to any issues that
arose. I thought this was best option for them.

Yet every time I asked my husband to look after the
youngest girl (only just three) he wouldn't come home,
or would come in from work and go straight out. And
so, the first week of the holidays passed.

'We need to tell the girls. It's only fair,' I pleaded
with him at the end of the first week of the holidays. 'If
we don't say something, they may hear from someone
else that the house is for sale.'

'It's your choice to end the marriage, you deal with it,' was all my husband would say.

'Can't we try to discuss this so we have a plan to help them and cause them the least amount of pain?' I replied.

'It's your choice, only you are causing the pain. It's nothing to do with me,' he said.

'Do you want them to find out about our divorce from someone else? Wouldn't it be better coming from us?' I asked.

'It's nothing to do with me. It's your choice, you deal with it,' he replied again.

During the second week of the holidays he wasn't around, despite my pleas for help. It took until the last day for me to realise he wasn't going to take part in the process. I waited for him to come into the house, then grabbed the two older girls and put them in the car. Leaving the house, I shouted to him to look after the youngest. Then I told the two older girls what was going to happen in the car park close to the local beach. There were no other options. I was shaking as I sat looking out to the sea.

'Daddy and I are going to get divorced,' I said, 'which means we're going to have to sell the house.' I looked at both of them, and instantly the middle child, six-years-old, started crying.

'I don't want you to stop being together,' she said over and over. 'I don't want you to not be married. Why can't you stay married? Why can't you stay together?' she sobbed.

'Mummy doesn't love daddy anymore, and so I can't stay married to him,' I replied.

My eldest, a deeply perceptive and emotional child of nine wanted to know more practical details.

'If you are going to look after us mummy, will you get a bigger share of the money we get for the house? That's only fair,' she asked.

'I don't know darling,' I answered. I had no answers for either child; so all I did was listen to them and try to calm their fears. 'Will we be able to go to the same school, Mummy?' asked my six-year-old. 'Where will we live?'

'Will we be able to see daddy?' asked my oldest daughter.

'You will definitely be able to go to the same school. I'm not sure exactly where we are going to live, but it won't be far from here. And you can still see daddy whenever you want to,' I said.

'But why can't you stay together?' asked my middle daughter again. 'I don't want you to leave daddy.'

'I can't stay with daddy forever if I don't love him anymore. It wouldn't be fair for him or me,' I said. 'Whatever happens, we four girls will always be together. And you will always be able to see daddy. Even though we won't be married it doesn't mean either of us doesn't love you anymore. We've just decided that mummy and daddy won't live together anymore.'

Children...they have that canny way of instantly adapting to the circumstances into which they are thrown, and by the time we had finished our conversation, and drove home they were already making sense of the situation. This isn't to say they didn't have a lot of questions. For me, the important thing was to give them only the answers they needed, which weren't always the ones they wanted.

Don't overload any child with information that is only suitable for adults. At that stage of their lives a lot of the replies had to consist of 'I don't know why this happens, sometimes it just does.' Repeatedly I reassured them it was nothing to do with them, and that both parents loved them. We four girls then had to wait to see what would happen next in our lives.

When I reached the decision to leave my marriage, I truly believed my husband and I would be able to agree on the best way to do this, and that we would be able to put the children first. I believed that we would go separate ways with their mental, emotional and physical welfare paramount for us both. Before we got married we had discussed what would happen if we ever decided to get divorce, and both of us had agreed that we would always put the children first, however painful that would be.

I was naïve. Maybe I was stupid. After I had told the girls I went out for a drink with my friend Louise, who was also divorced. There was literally no one else to talk to who could give me some guidance. I will never forget the first thing she said to me: 'Things will get a lot worse before they get better.'

I had only 'endured' the first few months of separation and I was at a physical and emotional low point. My weight had dropped to just under seven stone. I was sleeping terribly. My anxiety levels were stratospheric. I would still describe this stage as full of terror. My main fear was what was going to happen to the girls? How was I going to support them, emotionally and financially, so that they could continue their journey through life? I had crazy notions of having to live in a tent or being homeless. For a little while I really didn't know where we would be living.

Yet deep inside me, whilst the fear and anxiety swirled about in my mind in a daily tempest, I was clear that even if the girls and I ended up with nowhere to live, we would still survive, because with each other, we could surmount each problem as it arrived. If you believe that your love for each other will get you through each problem, then it will. A field and a tent. If that became our reality, then we would adapt. I practised my daily mantras, focusing positive energy religiously on gaining work. With little energy to spare for running I started swimming every week.

At home the situation deteriorated in a way I couldn't have contemplated. As the weeks continued to pass, the girls' dad continued to ignore them. Again and again I confronted him about how wrong this was and told him that he was taking out his anger on them to punish me. My pleas to him to talk to the children or spend time with them, were always disregarded. I tried to cover up his behaviour by saying he was busy at work, and always tired. I also tried to compensate for this difficult and unforeseen circumstance, by keeping the children's activities going, by giving them the chance to speak openly about their feelings - just maintaining the 'normality' of daily life. I was also getting more regular work, as well as trudging through the many forms that had to be filled in due to my new status.

No one can foresee how draining the bureaucracy of divorce can be. Mediation, by its nature, requires many financial documents to be collated from both parties. Statements from all bank accounts, loans, mortgage and pay slips. If you are the party who is leaving the marriage, perhaps it is best to expect to have to do all of this yourself on behalf of both parties. Applying for Children's Tax Credits and Working Family Tax Credits also requires a lot of form filling.

The benefits system is always changing, so please check out what benefits you may be entitled to at the time you read this book.

Finding the hours and the energy to do everything that is needed can be tough, especially if you have young children. If you are exhausted it's hard to motivate yourself to cope with such painstaking forms, but it's a necessary evil to help move forward the slow process that is divorce. I would often look at the pile of forms, cry, and then try to do one or two pages. If friends can help by taking your children out so you can take time to focus, it can be a much quicker process. The most important thing is to keep doing what you need to do every day, so that you can see some progress.

This was a time when I really needed my friends to help me out on a day-to-day basis. More importantly -

and this is such a cliché - it was at this stage that I learnt who my true friends were. Just a small handful of friends were ready to step in and make a roast dinner when I had no energy left, or pick up the children from school so that I could attend mediation.

I am now a firm believer that we all only need a small handful of true friends who will help us to face life's challenges, so having even one person out there who will listen and help despite their own busy lives, is a lifeline that can keep you going. I was lucky as I had several. Other people asked how I was coping or if I needed help, and they provided extra support that made a huge difference. Members of my family helped when they could as well, especially with the girls. This is a time that you need to call on your family and friends. And I know you will also find out who they really are. Let them help you, and one day you will be able to return their gift. This is such a valuable insight and one blessing from such a difficult experience.

One of the best time-management techniques that I found, and to which I stuck religiously, was to make a list at the end of each day of five 'must do' jobs. Instead of making 'to do' lists everyday, with many items you are never going to be able to tick off, this teaches you to spend five minutes every evening thinking about what's really important for the next day. One person can't work, fill in endless forms, look after multiple children and manage a house without a system that helps them feel they are in control.

If you have a really busy day or a really bad day, and only manage two or three of your items, the remaining ones can be moved to your list for the next day. Avoid that feeling of being constantly overwhelmed by everything that needs to be done by focusing specifically on what is urgent for the next day. When you tick off your five items you will have a greater sense of achievement than running around trying to do everything and ending up burnt out each evening.

Another essential strategy to help you cope with everyday life is to ensure your kids are on board and helping you with some of the daily chores and housework. By the time my youngest was three-years-old she would help me unload the dishwasher, clean out the fire, and even clean the bathroom with me! If flashbacks to a Dickensian era have sprung to mind, I should add that I never made her do these things! These were the chores she found she liked (she is a very practical and earthy young lady!) and therefore, those that I asked her to help with. We all have chores that we absolutely hate; so my suggestion is for you to find ones that are tolerable for each child as they are more likely to do it without moaning and groaning about it so much that you give up asking them just to avoid a verbal battle! Even now, six years on, we put on some loud music on a Friday evening, share out the chores between us and reward ourselves with watching something on the television together once they are done.

It's essential if you have delegated some jobs or chores that you don't criticise your children's work or redo the job. Once you accept that a child will never do a job in the same way as an adult, you are on your way to being grateful for whatever contribution they make. Your house may not be sparkling clean, but by job sharing you can tackle your domestic chores as a team. I hate doing housework on my own so I really am thankful for the help and I praise any help that is given. No job is too small to be praised! It will make your kids feel they are helping you, which is important for them, too.

* * *

Hopefully your family will be an essential means of support during this time. Family members can be a godsend, helping with babysitting, making meals, giving hugs at just the right moment and providing the love you need to power through the tough times. Though for some of you, there may not be the family support you expect or hope for, and this can come as a shock. For some family members, their own feelings may get in the way of being able to outwardly express the love you may need.

It's possible that your separation may come as a shock to your family and if your family doesn't agree with your decision it can be hard for you to watch them giving support to your partner rather than to you. Some family members may wish to remain neutral, supporting both partners who are separating. If this happens, or if your family is giving your partner more support than you, you may feel isolated, abandoned and deeply hurt. Do people take sides in divorce or times of conflict? They shouldn't, and we all hope that we ourselves wouldn't, but many do.

Ultimately, none of us can control anyone else's actions, so if you feel the support you need is not forthcoming from your family, you may need to turn to other sources to receive help. This could be your local church, your General Practitioner, online networks and forums or your friends. If you are going through a really tough experience, the reactions of your family can be bewildering and impossible to understand. If an important family member withholds support for you, you'll feel as if you're going through two divorces at the same time. If a relative has gone through a similar experience to yours, your divorce may trigger their own feelings of grief and sadness about their own past.

But this is your divorce, and you have to focus on getting through it, rather than allow the words or actions of others to distract or dominate your thoughts. You have to believe that somehow and from somewhere, you will receive the help you need.

* * *

As my separation progressed - slowly and painfully - I carried on, trying to keep up with everything that needed to be done. There were times that I almost considered 'giving in', or should I say 'caving in' to the pressures being put on me by going back to the marriage in order to end the feelings of despair. It would have been an easier solution in some ways, but I refused to get back together with a man I didn't love, just for the sake of the children.

The person who had not been a part of my life for all of my twenties had been my dad, but now he had come back into my life, and it was he who would step in to be the rock that I could lean on at what felt like a disastrous time.

I didn't see my dad much when I was a child, and I don't have any memories of him being at home, not just because my parents were divorced, but my dad was a submariner in the Royal Navy, so he spent considerable periods abroad or at sea. We did see him, but not very often. When I was about 11, my brother went to live with my dad while I stayed with my mum. By the time my brother was 18, my dad believed it was time for my brother to move out and support himself. Apparently, this wasn't an unusual belief for my father's generation, and indeed, my dad had himself joined the Navy when he was 15. This was a shock for my brother and for my sister and me as well; and anyway, we were all incredibly vulnerable due to our own experience of growing up with divorced parents. My dad had remarried, and my brother had lived with my step-mum and her two children.

I can remember sending my dad a letter when I was coming to the end of my time at university and asking him to help me fund my way through my Masters degree, but he told me he couldn't. He couldn't afford to help me because his step-children were now his financial responsibility. Neither my sister, nor my brother or I could understand how he could put someone else's children before us. We all felt dismay that we weren't his priority, and I know we were all incredibly hurt. I didn't reply to the letter and I didn't hear from him again, although eventually I heard through my step-sister that my dad and step-mum had moved to South Africa.

The years flew by as I carried on my studies then established myself as a journalist in London. However, when I was pregnant with my first child I traced my dad in South Africa to tell him he was going to be a granddad. It was really important to me that he acknowledged his granddaughter, probably because I had felt so abandoned during my own childhood, which impressed upon me the need for my children to know who all the members of their family were. Despite over 10 years of not seeing him, and the distance that now lay between us, when we first talked on Skype it was as if we had never had any time apart. It wasn't long before he visited the UK to see us, and over the next couple of years it was wonderful to have him in my life again. When my marriage began to unravel, it was my dad I turned to for help.

Fundamentally he was a positive, outgoing, energetic person. Sitting Skyping across the African continent he listened, and being a military man, his motto to me was to take my grief out on the road. Through his own divorce and for the years he spent on his own thereafter, running became his therapy, and it perhaps was inevitable that it would become mine. In his eyes and mine, falling apart just wasn't an option. Children and their emotional security, prohibit such behaviour.

I couldn't stop running for long anyway as it was so much a part of my daily and weekly existence. Yet I didn't have a babysitter to leave the girls with, which would have allowed me to go to my club's sessions. It didn't matter. I found a local field and would get the girls to play in the middle while I ran around the outside or I took them to the park and ran around its perimeter for as long as I could until they got bored or started fighting. We even did this in January, with the girls lasting for as long as they could before the cold nipped into their bones. By bringing this routine back into my life, my energy returned and I regained a vital sense of perspective. Running became my meditation, and it helped my mind to settle and clear. It gave me a break from the confusing thoughts and it made me feel stronger.

At this time of my life my dad gave me his biggest gift - that of listening. Despairing sobs couldn't last long because his humour and positive outlook buoyed me up time and again when I felt there was no one else to turn to or who would listen. 'Hold your head high,' was his mantra to me, as well as in true, stiff-upper-lip military style, 'Carry on.'

Suggestions

Look online for some of the great books that can help your child cope with divorce or separation. Some of our favourites were *Was it the chocolate pudding?* and *It's not your fault Koko bear.* There are also many adult reference books that can guide you in putting your children first – my personal favourite, which I have lent to other mums, was *Putting children first: A handbook for separated parents* by Karen Woodall (£12.99, Piatkus).

- If you have children, can both parties agree to make a plan about how and when you are going to tell them about your separation and divorce? Experts recommend we only tell children what they need to know, and not what they want to know. Give them the information they need and follow this up with reassurance that they are not to blame, and assure them that they are loved and secure. With this reassurance children will adapt surprisingly quickly to changing circumstances.
- Follow this up by giving your children time to talk, if they need it. When you are walking to school or the park, or if you are in the car, ask them what is

happening in their lives. Don't try and lead the conversation – whatever they chose to share with you listen to it, repeat it back, and feel grateful they have chosen to share some of their feelings.

- Every evening make a list of five 'must do' jobs that need to be done the next day. This will focus your mind on what is really important and achievable.

- If you have many forms to fill in seek help. Many of us feel dread when faced with forms, especially if they require financial information. Setting yourself daily targets of gathering a certain amount of information can see you progress towards achieving your goal. Expecting to fill in your forms all at once or hiding them out of sight and avoiding them, will not only slow down your progress, it will cause you to stagnate in negative emotions. Set yourself a target, and ask for help if you need it.

- Once they are old enough, delegate some of the everyday chores to each of your children. You can make this fun by writing them on a piece of paper and drawing them from a hat. If you use the words: 'I really need your help to…' you are asking them to support you, rather than telling them what to do. Make sure you all get a reward at the end, and praise any help you get! This will also boost your kids' self-esteem.

- At times, family and friends often take sides, even if they don't realise it or don't intend to cause pain by doing so. They may be struggling with their own repressed emotions or memories. Try to focus on yourself, or let other people come into your life to help you when you need it. Cherish those who will listen to you – it is a wonderful gift.

- Don't let your own anger or the anger of others overcome you. Deflect the anger of others – recognising it is more about them than about you – and focus on more positive emotions. Others can't make you feel bad about yourself as only you can allow this. Praise yourself for making your way through each stage of divorce. As you experience the volcanic and passionate emotions of divorce firsthand, your internal emotional landscape will never be the same again. We can't control other's actions, feelings or emotions, but we can control our own. One of my daily mantras was: 'I am strong, I am brave, I am happy.' This is one experience you are going through on a very long journey through life. When you are in your eighties and look back at your life, there's a good chance you won't remember many of the details of this time, even though they are painful to experience right now.

Step Three to a New You

Now more than ever it's time to dig out some trainers, lace them up and get out and run, as this will help you channel and release your emotions. Whatever energy you put into sport, you get far more back.

- If you're still finding your running feet, try following the NHS Live Well Couch to 5K training plan **(www.nhs.uk/livewell/c25k),** which is a nine-week running plan for beginners. Do something positive right now for you! If you have managed to get out already, now you need to aim to train two to three times a week. Make one run a slightly longer distance, where you run at a slow enough pace that enables you to chat with a friend at the same time. On the other run, do a 10-minute slow jog warm up then run three-five short hills, recovering slowly on the way down, followed by a 10-minute warm down. Alternatively, do a 10-minute warm up followed by running fast for one minute, followed by a 60-second recovery, repeating five to ten times depending on how you feel. Finish with a 10-minute slow jog warm down. If you prefer swimming or cycling, you can do the same session in your chosen activity.

Go to the Appendix for my beginner's 10-week training plan.

- If this feels too challenging, why not find a local park to jog around? After a gentle jog to warm up, run fast along one side then walk the next, repeating for 10 minutes. Get your kids to switch off their screens and come with you as they can play, run with you or ride their bikes.

Spend five minutes writing down three challenging tasks that you have recently tackled, and note down the way in which you overcame them. After each one write, 'I am thankful and grateful for…' (Include either a person or an emotion that helped you succeed).

....

....

....

....

....

....

CHAPTER FOUR

'Take the first step in faith. You don't have to see the whole staircase. Just take the first step.'
Dr Martin Luther King

Bricks and Mortar

Our house went on the market at Easter and it sold straight away but it was to take until July for the sale to be finalised. My husband and I were still living together but hardly talking, and this carried on for six months after we agreed to separate. At Easter I knew I would need to start looking for somewhere for the girls and myself to live. Was selling the family home a terrible experience? As it turned out, selling the house was the best thing that happened to me at that time.

We had thought we would be moving house during the summer of 2010, yet by a strange twist of fate, the people who bought our home decided to rent it out and they asked me to stay on as a tenant. This gave the girls the breathing space they needed in which to get used to their new way of life. The bricks and mortar stayed the same, but their dad left that summer. During the first week of the summer holidays we visited my sister, and when we returned, he was gone and I finally became a single mum.

At this time we were in dire financial straights. For quite a long time we lived on absolutely nothing and I didn't buy the girls clothes for over a year. My sole focus was keeping their lives going – working hard at school, enjoying their after-school activities, and trying to be the mum they needed. For the whole of the first year after separation I was fuelled by adrenaline. My fight or flight response was in - well, full flight! I also didn't drink any alcohol and I didn't socialise in the traditional way. My bedtime would be early, though sometimes anxiety would prevent sleep until the early hours of the morning. I used meditation to calm the worries that popped into my mind and to relax my body. Doing an evening yoga class or having a body massage from a friend later in the day also helped me relax.

For the first year I did everything possible to keep the girls' lives 'normal'. I had little money and therefore was allowed the gift of looking at life, and of living it, without any financial security. Looking back, this was one of the greatest blessings of my divorce. A house is just bricks and mortar, and having money gives you no guarantee of happiness or love. I knew I didn't want to stay in an unhappy relationship for the sake of bricks and mortar.

Yet the simplest things - the children's laughter, a friend's hug that crushes your bones, an emotive song playing on the radio at just the right moment - became my new currency. When we are told as children that having less can mean living more, we often don't grasp the depth of meaning that our elders are trying to share. Since separation I have never felt so rich, as the unconditional love I receive brings more happiness than any mortgage, wardrobe full or clothes or new car ever could.

Friends rallied round to give me the practical items as well as the emotional support that I needed. At this time I also turned to hypnotherapy to help my mind assimilate a new way of life, which required changing standards. My hypnotherapist, Lynda Panter, had guided me through the complicated birth of my third daughter, and I would return to her over the next few years when I found the issues that I was dealing with too much to cope with. One session with her would re-instil calm and allow me to see the way forward more clearly. Lynda was able to address my fears and worries and she encouraged me to believe in myself, and to gain the inner strength that I needed in order to survive the experience. More than a hypnotherapist, she became a life coach who I visited every time the pressures got too much and I felt I couldn't cope.

Running also took an upturn. For me, running was the greatest antidote to stress, and the greatest aphrodisiac I could take to help me fall back in love with my life. I became a creature of habit, hunting out some green space to give me instant access to the restorative powers of Mother Nature. Glimpsing a fox or catching the sound of a distant woodpecker would instantly pour energy back into my soul. It gave me the spiritual energy that I needed to cope with everything I was going through. For all of us, including me, the progress you make with running can reflect back your returning strength. It can put you in touch with your inner strength more easily than the bottom of any wine bottle can do.

I found running became a marker for each stage of the divorce experience. At first I struggled to do anything at all, and then I began to set myself small goals. I set myself the goal of a 5K race in three months, a 10K race in six and maybe a marathon in 12. Each race I worked towards seemed to reflect to me that I was reaching my own personal turning points as I travelled the divorce road.

Reaching one, two then three miles when you are out running can represent the steps you are taking in empowering yourself once more. The goal of a race, whether it's a local five kilometre parkrun, Race for Life, 5K or 10K or even longer, can give you and your loved ones reassurance that you are regaining control of your life. In the back of my mind I began to think about the marathon that I had previously entered and failed to complete, a sure sign that life was turning round.

Even though our home had been sold, we hadn't lost the place in which we lived. My husband decided to live with friends about four miles away, but over the next two years the girls would only see him three times. For the first few years post separation, I invested as much energy and time as I could to ensure that some form of relationship between the girls and their dad continued. I would email updates on their progress at school or at activities, and photocopy their school reports. The girls wrote cards and letters and they made pictures for him. Yet he never gave us his address. I could have carried on doing this year in and year out, but eventually I decided to stop.

When a time comes when the girls want to know and to understand more deeply why their dad decided to walk away from their lives, I won't have the answers. I had to stop trying to encourage him to acknowledge the girls, and re-focus on positive people instead.

Losing your home or having to deal with complicated and unwanted situations makes you face your own fears and insecurities, and it forces you to deal with them. There's a good chance that anger is the emotion behind many of your feelings of others. While holding on to anger is pointless, we all do it to some extent. As we can't control the actions, feelings or emotions of others, there's a good chance they can feel unfair to us. We can focus on what we can control, which are our own feelings and emotions. As time passes this becomes easier to do. Finding a way to do this, either through some form of therapy or talking to friends about your feelings, can make the difference between coming through divorce feeling like a victim or a survivor.

Every mediation meeting we had was dreadful and whatever was up for discussion, my husband returned to the same caveat: 'You're splitting up the family; it's nothing to do with me.'

'Would you be able to see your daughters over the school holidays?' the mediator asked him as we tried to discuss shared childcare.

'No. I work,' he replied.

'Is it possible to share the repayments on the car loan so your wife can keep the car, as she has the three children to look after?' she then asked my husband.

'She's splitting the family, she has to pay,' was his reply.

'Would you be willing to split the costs of some of the after-school activities, so the children can keep them up?' the mediator then asked.

'No. She's split the family. I hope they end up living in a council house with lots of druggies,' my husband replied over and over again, each time his words were even more heavily loaded with anger.

Whatever the mediator asked, whether it was about financial, practical or emotional issues, my husband's reply was the same: 'She's done this. It's nothing to do with me. She can sort out the children.'

After several sessions it was obvious that we were going nowhere and I was simply turning up to give my husband another chance to attack me. Each attack was very personal, so I tried to concentrate on the children. I also worked on establishing some form of ongoing communication with their dad, but I failed.

We agreed maintenance payments would start once the house sale had gone through. I envisaged the house would be sold in July, the mediation would be finished and our solicitors would distribute the funds from the house and then maintenance would start. This didn't happen.

Mediation came to a close about the same time as the house sale went through, but when I presented our documentation to my solicitor, she told me our agreement wasn't fair towards the girls and me.

'You've taken on all the debts,' the solicitor pointed out when we were examining the mediation documentation.

These weren't massive; it was just money we had borrowed for do-it-yourself and a car loan.

'You've agreed to a percentage of the house sale money that doesn't reflect your role as the main carer for three children,' she added. 'My job is to ensure you receive the agreement that gives you and your children, the most security. This agreement doesn't do that.'

'My husband isn't willing to negotiate on these issues,' I replied, crumpled in a chair in her office. 'He refused to discuss these matters at mediation, he refused to bring any of the documentation we both needed to supply, and in the end I agreed to his terms. I just wanted it to be over so we could move on. Each meeting he was nasty about who I am. I couldn't get past this. It was impossible to reach any kind of agreement on all the different aspects we discussed.'

For me, mediation was a horrific experience, and in order for it to be over, I was willing to compromise. From a legal standpoint, I had compromised too far, and it took another year for my husband's and my solicitors to come to an agreement over the division of the profit of the house sale, and the splitting of other financial assets (which were few).

* * *

Looking back, I can see that the girls' behaviour was deeply affected by their dad leaving the family home that July. When my husband and I had first decided to separate I had visited their schools to inform them of the change in our situation, and I appealed to them for help. The schools were a great source of support. There was one person who stepped in to help us though, and she was the parental liaison officer for the cluster of schools, primary to secondary, in our village. Her name was Lisa Dalglish, and she became our very own fairy godmother.

Lisa gave me endless advice over the next few years and she is still doing so today. Her help has been immeasurable, as whatever obstacle I came up against, whether it was regarding my divorce, the girls' behaviour, their health, researching outside agencies regarding their emotional welfare – Lisa had the resources I needed. Every wall I came up against, she diverted me towards a clearer pathway.

Every school should have an Emotional Literacy Support Assistant (ELSA). These work to support the emotional needs of their pupils, recognising that children learn better and are happier in school if their emotional needs are also addressed. You can make an appointment at your school with one of these assistants so you can discuss between you the issues that have developed, which may include any behaviour that is causing worry, while offering strategies to support the child during school hours. As soon as my children knew about our separation I visited their respective schools to discuss what was happening at home and how the girls had reacted. Both schools offered considerable support to the girls, and their ELSAs and teachers kept me informed of any worries and concerns, so we could work together on allowing them to feel safe and confident in expressing their feelings. My middle daughter carried on talking regularly to her ELSA throughout all her years in junior school, and she built a strong relationship of trust with her. Her ELSA became someone she could confide in who wasn't at home and who wasn't involved in the divorce, and through individual one-on-one sessions she was given priceless time with an unbiased, kind and caring adult whose only focus was allowing her to express how she felt – be it good or bad.

It soon became clear that the girls' dad wasn't going to be a regular part of their lives. Lisa gave us strategies to deal with this, options to try in order to encourage open communication, and hope that the future would get better. It wasn't just the loss of a father figure that had an impact on all of our lives. One of my best friends, Mel, left the country to live in Australia. She had held my hand through the initial stages of separation. It was Mel who had drawn up a spreadsheet for me to show me that I could financially support the girls on my own. Heavenly dinners, piled high with root vegetables, were provided during lonely weekends when most friends were spending time with their own families. We were always welcome. Mel believed that I was strong enough to survive divorce, and she made me believe this too.

Then my oldest friend Caroline moved to New York. With both gone, I had to cope alone and yet they remained a magical lifeline. As my life became more about the behind-the-scenes work of holding together our family, finding and growing work, they both kept my spirit buoyed up from afar. A closer friend, Marina, was always on hand to take the girls to school if I was ill, and she gave practical help when I needed it. Three strong women were there for me, whatever I needed.

For months it seemed as though separation progressing into divorce was never going to happen. After mediation finished it took a year before both sets of solicitors were happy with our financial settlement. This year was tough and draining. This is the stage where you just want everything to end so that you can move on but this never seemed to come. Delays were endless, and each step was a bureaucratic marathon. Without divorce I was unable to access the money that the sale of our house had left us. All four of us lived a very frugal few years, though the girls were too young to realise.

During the first year we lived alone, as tenants, in our old family home, I worked. I didn't go out at all. Once the children were in bed it was time to write and that became my mission, as it was up to me to support them. I was keen to write for running magazines and I pitched ideas to several editors. David Castle, author and editor of Running Fitness took a chance on me and gave me some work. He liked what I did and soon I was a regular writer and columnist for the magazine.

Just over a year after I had separated I headed to the London Marathon Expo to help out on the Running Fitness stand and I finally met David. We were in a similar position, as he was also going through separation at that time. I loved working for the magazine, whether I was shooting off to races which I was to review, testing kit or being a human guinea pig trialling running experiences. David and I couldn't have been more alike, both being runners and writers, and both passionate about our sport. I found out that David studied Sport Science at Loughborough University. I had applied to do the same course, the same year but I had been rejected. It felt as though we were destined to be together, but at the right time in both our lives, which just happened to be at the time of our 40th birthdays.

Nearly two years after separating from my husband, and over a year after the girls and I had started living alone in our family home, David and I moved in together – in a house in the same village. On top of being a dad to two children, his heart was large enough to love my three girls as well. We became a blended family (which can bring its own complications) and it became one that would become as strong as a steel fortress.

The Child Support Agency

There came a time when I had to contact the Child Support Agency (CSA), just prior to our decree absolute, to set in motion maintenance payments. As there was no contact between my husband and me, sorting out maintenance payments between ourselves obviously wasn't going to happen. This started another set of bureaucratic procedures that seemed as complicated as all the others I had taken on post separation.

The CSA, and Child Maintenance Service (CMS), exists for those parents who are unable to agree their child maintenance between themselves. You don't need to use the CSA to arrange child maintenance, and many parents are able to agree theirs between themselves – this is called a family-based arrangement. Parents arrange everything themselves and no one else has to be involved. The CSA can provide impartial information on how to do this. Some parents also agree their maintenance payments via their solicitors, without involving the CSA.

There are times when neither of the above are options, and the CSA can help if you need to find the other parent, sort out disagreements about parentage, work out how much child maintenance should be paid and pass payments to the 'receiving' parent (who has the main day-to-day care of the child). The CSA will look at the payments whenever there are any changes in the parents' circumstances, review the payment amount every year, and take action if payments aren't made. With the introduction in 2014 of application fees and enforcement charges, parents are encouraged to work out their own family-based arrangements.

The CSA has received some bad press over the years, but my advice is simple. If a government body is handling your case and is helping you to receive maintenance, you have to keep on top of your progress if you want to ensure that you get your payments. If you've never had any dealings with the CMS or CSA you may be unaware that, just as you have to stand your ground to get an appointment at your doctor's surgery, you may have to ring, badger, and demand and bully them to make sure they are dealing with your case!

Our case somehow fell by the wayside. I waited. I waited more and then I rang them. They insisted they were trying to sort out the case and they may have been, but this took months, and even then, when they informed me that they would be taking maintenance from my ex-husband, the amount they took for the first few months was well below the amount they declared he should pay. Again I chased them, and finally, I received a full maintenance payment. This happened two years after we had separated! Then I received another one... and then I received a letter to tell me there would be no more payments. At this stage I crumpled.

The morning I received my notification from the CSA of the ceasing of all maintenance payments I rang them for more information. Supportive though they were, they couldn't help me. All they knew was that my ex-husband had notified them that he had left his job.

It had taken so much energy to get to this stage (I was still waiting for my decree absolute, which would mark the official end of the marriage). I had been completely unaware how slow moving the bureaucracy of divorce would be, or how many obstacles would have to be endlessly overcome.

I wouldn't have believed it possible, but the next year would prove to be even more complicated, and much harder, than the previous two. Again I felt I was spiralling back down into a dark place. The question I would have to ask myself over and over, was whether I could fight my way back to a better place.

Suggestions

Make contact with your children's schools and teachers to advise them of the situation at home. They will support your child and keep you informed of any changes in behaviour that cause concern. Find out if your school has an Emotional Literacy Support Assistant (ELSA), or similar and make an appointment with one of them to discuss your concerns.

• Contact the Child Support Agency:

(**www.gov.uk/child-maintenance**) and use their child maintenance calculator, if you need help with establishing financial support for your children.

- Meditation is a tool you can take anywhere. You don't need to love yoga or be a Buddhist to benefit from it. By putting your mind on your breath (concentrating on breathing rather than the endless thoughts that spring up in your mind) you can calm your heartbeat and allow peace into your day. Even five minutes a day will make you feel more in control of your mind, allowing you to focus more on what you need and want to do. I meditate mainly when running, which helps both my mind and my asthmatic lungs, but you can do it at the kitchen sink as well as at your desk. You don't have to carve out time to be alone, although if you can you will feel more benefit.

- If money is tight be creative! Charity shops, second-hand uniform sales and EBay provide choice and everything your child needs at a reduced price. Find activities for your children that are free. Traditional pastimes like going to the library, the park, the woods, and the beach or on a bike ride work along with a homemade picnic. Getting out of the house, back to nature, and mucking around with your kids will enrich all of your souls.

- Tackle stress, anxiety, depression and grief with a two-pronged approach. Firstly, take up some form of exercise such as yoga, Pilates or jogging. Endorphins are our own feel-good hormones and they can be very powerful. Once you get through the initial shock of returning to exercise, your body will reward you with the cheapest and most natural high in the world. Look into complementary therapies such as Reiki, hypnotherapy, homeopathy, aromatherapy, Tai chi and acupuncture (plus many, many more) as these can help you cope with some of the difficult feelings and emotions you experience.

Step Four to a New You

Now you're regularly running three times a week, it's time to consider entering a race! Don't panic, this is more about putting a date in your calendar for the not-so-distant future. It can be as short as your local free parkrun **(www.parkrun.co.uk)**, a friendly Race for Life 5 or 10K - see:

- **(www. raceforlife.cancerresearchuk.org)** or one of the non-threatening, family-friendly Women's Running 10K Series:

  (www.womensrunninguk.co.uk) that are held throughout the country. Or maybe you fancy something longer? Do your research, find the right race for you, find a beginner's 10K training plan online and enter. Tell your friends about it. This will help you commit to training. If you haven't, consider joining your local running club as you will get support, encouragement and endless motivation from members (and you may just make some friends for life).

- If this feels too challenging, why not see how your running is progressing by setting yourself a personal time-trial? Measure a course around your local streets – anything from a mile to three miles – and simply run it as fast as you can! If this is your first time running at pace, make sure you gauge your effort – if you're out of breath after 60 seconds, it's going to be a painful experience. Think positively – you may never have imagined you could do this. Now you really have something to measure your progress!

Spend five minutes writing down three goals you would like to achieve, whether it is domestic, personal, educational etc.

Start each sentence with: 'I am ....'

Imagine what it feels like to achieve these goals, especially when you go to bed at night!

....

....

....

CHAPTER FIVE

*'A mind preoccupied with thoughts of resentment and
bitterness cannot change the past. Nor do those thoughts
wound anyone but the soul that beholds them.'*
DODINSKY

After more than two years, my husband re-contacted
me. He wanted to see the girls regularly - every
other weekend if possible. The girls were ecstatic! All
they wanted was to be acknowledged by their dad and
they were so excited to see him on that first meeting.
My middle daughter had felt very angry towards me
for leaving the marriage, and I think the youngest,
confused by her feelings, would often copy her big
sister in these behaviours. They all came back full of
excitement after seeing him and it was amazing to see
them so happy!

Their dad told them he would see them again in two
weekends, and again, they couldn't be happier.
However, no formal arrangements were made, and the
day came and went and he didn't reply to my texts
about seeing the girls. Then he did get in contact. Then
he made an arrangement but did not keep it. Obviously,
this was causing the girls and me some anxiety. Two
years down the line you have no more excuses or 'white
lies' that you can tell to protect their feelings. Again, he
contacted me asking to see them. Wary as I was, I was
still naively expecting some sort of informal
arrangement to develop but on that meeting, he told the

girls he was moving abroad so he wouldn't be able to see them again. He would be living in Australia.

How did they behave that day? Bizarrely would probably be the best word. They came back from their visit with the news, sad but happy because daddy was doing the right thing for himself. Each had been given a parting gift – an old book, a childhood teddy and a game. And that, it seemed, was that.

The first impact of this news was that the two youngest daughters became even angrier with me, as it was my fault that their daddy was leaving them again. Emotions and feelings, were either being buried deep (the eldest) or exploding (the middle daughter), or just seeping out in private sobs (the youngest).

Family and friends all worked together to reassure their young minds. The Internet, Skype, FaceTime; there are endless opportunities for contact regardless of where you live. Can any child go through such an experience without some kind of emotional backlash? During the new few months it felt as though we had been cast adrift in very rocky seas, but we were thrown several lifelines, and it would be these that I had to hold on to very strongly.

By this stage it was clear that the girls all had very different interpretations of the events that had happened to them. They were all unique, and such strange and wonderful creatures – but cracks in our lives were starting to show. I think throughout the whole separation period I had expected outward, open, 'in-your-face' displays of anger and pain but this wasn't always the case. Sometimes the hardest pain reveals itself in the subtlest of ways. My eldest didn't (and still won't) want to talk about her feelings. This initially caused me more worry than if she had been shouting that she hated me. Lisa Dalglish taught me to let her share her emotions when she was ready – and that if she never chose to do this, than that would be the right

Chapter Five

decision for her. The middle girl was the opposite, being very vociferous and condemning in her words.

'I hate you!' she would shout at me, almost daily. 'If you hadn't left daddy he wouldn't be moving away. It's all your fault!'

I tried to talk to her but she would feel so cross she would hit me. Occasionally she hit me from behind on my back, and being a strong girl this hurt and it brought tears to my eyes.

'That is not acceptable,' I would tell her.

'I don't care, it's your fault daddy is moving away! We won't be able to see him because of you!' she screamed. If I tried to talk about how her dad's decisions were his, not mine, she would just scream louder at me.

Emotions and anger spilled over into her daily life, and to help her gain some control she received support at school. My youngest, and most eccentric, girl relied on her imaginary friend, Marvin, to prop her up, but she also copied a lot of the behaviours of her big sister. Both would hit me when they felt really frustrated. I couldn't blame them.

Expect anger, which may bubble over into physical aggression. When this happens instantly explain to your children that their behaviour is inappropriate, reassuring them that there are other ways to express their emotions. Always try to end difficult situations by explaining to your children that their feelings are natural, but they must find a way to express them in a way that doesn't hurt other people. Tell them, over and over, that the separation or divorce has nothing to do with them, and that both parents love them very much. I told my girls this over and over again.

Find ways for your children to channel this grief. I stuck to what I knew best, so I started encouraging my middle daughter to go for a run with me, even for four or five minutes. We would lace up our trainers and jog around the block, and just five minutes would be enough to enable her to release the feelings that overwhelmed her. She would shout and snap at me all the way round but it still helped her. Another strategy we used was writing down feelings on a piece of paper then folding it up as small as we could and throwing it into the sea.

A referral to our local Child and Adolescent Mental Health Service provided everyone with what they needed most, the chance to have their voice heard by all members of the family. Family therapy, though difficult, is a powerful tool for acceptance and change. It was many things for me: daunting, exhausting, draining, confrontational, healing and unifying.

All of us had the opportunity to talk about how we felt; how we were struggling and our sadness. It was almost impossible at some meetings, as I was faced with the children's reluctance to talk, and natural alliance to the parent who was missing. Both the counsellor and I encouraged the girls to share their thoughts but they didn't come pouring out. It took a few sessions before any of the girls felt they could talk, as if they were worried they would be punished for their feelings. Understandably they saw the separation as the cause of their dad's decision to move away. I had initiated the separation; therefore I was responsible for their dad's behaviour. To them, he didn't need to take any responsibility for the way he was behaving. More simply put (in children's terminology): 'It's all your fault.'

The children had no means of contacting their dad; no forwarding address or phone number, no agreement to talk on the phone regularly or to Skype each other. They had little to grasp on to, and blaming me was the easiest way to express their anger. Yet those precious sessions were where we talked together about the way that none of us are responsible for another person's decisions and actions. The sessions were where they were able to speak truthfully about how sad and angry they felt about their dad moving country, and this gave us all the opportunity to heal. I learnt to listen to them. Truly listen. To ask them how their day went, and listen to their replies. To not ask questions for my own benefit or to settle my own anxieties.

It took a long time, but as the months passed we all slowly started to accept the new world we inhabited, a world which their dad was no longer part of. The girls were now in the same position I had been in as a child, with their dad living abroad. There was no communication between them and their dad, but therapy gave them the chance to talk about their feelings. After several months it seemed like they were starting to accept what had happened, and it was then that the opportunity for us all to visit my dad in South Africa came up, and after such a tough six months I knew we had to go.

The beauty and diversity of South Africa! It was a golden time for our family, three precious weeks full of adventure, sunshine, beautiful, interesting, intense countryside, flora, fauna, creatures... new friends, children running free, happy, curious, expressive, brown as berries.

My dad was frail but he became buoyed up, bristling with happiness as his granddaughters shared his days and strayed back to him, over and over, for the cuddles they needed. Despite being in pain, and having to use a portable oxygen cylinder, he insisted on taking us on safari, to see the natural wonders of beautiful South Africa, his second home. I was granted the opportunity to talk to my dad about my childhood, his past, and our family. I slowly filled in the holes of my past. There were some difficult memories to talk about; especially about my parents' divorce when I was the same age as my youngest daughter was on that trip.

Forever the historian, I strayed back to his childhood in our conversations, trying to uncover the details of his family. Each conversation was precious. If the girls gave me a hard time (which, of course they did!) he would stop them and ask them to think. Mainly we laughed about the curious and almost ridiculous nature of life.

On the day of our departure my dad's health deteriorated once again and I had to say goodbye to him in the local intensive care unit. Flying back to England we were regenerated and happy. My step-mum assured me my dad would recover.

As family therapy came to an end, and our tans soon faded in the harsh cold of England in January and February, I got ill. A chest infection wouldn't shift and a urinary tract infection revealed how run down I had become. For three years I had drawn on all of my reserves to keep life as normal as possible for the children. A crash, perhaps, was inevitable.

My urinary infection quickly became a kidney infection and it took a week in hospital to get my core temperature back down to normal. When you are in so much pain you don't really worry about who will be looking after your children or making sure they are all right, but I was fortunate that David, with help from my family, took control of looking after the girls. Hospital was awful. Like everyone else who spends more than a day in one, all I wanted was to get home. Even when the antibiotics started to control the infection and I could think about getting home, it took weeks before I felt well enough to get out of bed and help with the girls. The illness left me unable to do anything. Having had sole responsibility for the girls for so long, this time was stressful. Without David's help, in both practical terms and encouraging me to believe I would get back on my feet and be okay, I would have fallen apart.

My dad phoned me a couple of times, trying to boost my spirits – even though he was in and out of hospital himself. He said he was really worried about me. I don't think he had ever told me this before. I knew

I would be all right eventually, and I told him I was also worried about him.

Spring was pushing its way through the soil and forcing its way out from behind the winter clouds, and slowly, week after week, my strength and resilience returned. March became April and after two months I returned to running, as always for my sanity more than anything.

When the Virgin Money London Marathon came round, I had a lazy morning in bed watching it on the television, as I did every year. My dad had been a great runner, and I had always shared his passion for running. He rang me whilst he was watching the marathon in South Africa, and we talked about how the race was unfolding, and how my aim was to get fit and strong again and to try for another marathon personal best that year. Later that day he collapsed and died.

Knowing that he had been ill for a long time, and that he'd been in and out of intensive care for six months, I knew it was going to happen. I felt conflicting emotions. On one level I felt freed from the emotions that I had experienced as a child which always revolved around loss and not having him around. With him no longer being alive there was no longer any need to hold on to these emotions. However, it wasn't long before selfish feelings of anger bubbled up into my mind. It was my dad who had stood by me during my separation and divorce. It was he who had listened to me, who hadn't judged me, and who offered words of support, over and over. I had to face it. I was cross with him for abandoning me when I still needed his support. I was still feeling the same emotions as I had as a child.

Of course, he became an internal presence, someone I could check in with every day and talk to without anyone knowing, spending any effort even on talking, and who just listened (and definitely didn't judge!). Not really knowing how to process my feelings I resolved to run a marathon in his memory. This inspired me to get fit and well. I thought, with my background, I would bounce back and be able to run my marathon that year, but in reality it would take over a year for me to recover and be able to stand at the start of a marathon once again.

During the summer of 2013, as I yo-yoed between feeling better then falling back into struggling with daily life, I also began another legal process. Having never been to court before, I had to appear in front of my county court to make an application to the Child Support Agency of Australia. On recommendation from the British Child Support Agency I had begun a process to apply for maintenance for the girls – which was to become another time-consuming, energy-sapping procedure.

If your ex-partner has moved country their new country of residence may have a reciprocal maintenance agreement with the UK. Reciprocal Enforcement of Maintenance Orders (REMO) is the process by which maintenance orders made by UK courts on behalf of UK residents can be registered and enforced by courts or other authorities in other countries against people resident there. A reciprocal arrangement is governed by international conventions, which means that foreign maintenance orders in favour of individuals abroad can likewise be registered and enforced by UK courts against UK residents.

The precise nature of reciprocity available between the UK and another jurisdiction depends on the convention or agreement to which the other country is a signatory. A UK resident who wishes to apply to obtain maintenance from a person overseas should approach their local magistrates' court (or county court where the order was made), whether they have an existing court order for maintenance or there is no existing order.

Procedures also exist to enable an applicant to ask the foreign authorities to create an order for maintenance on their behalf.

There is no need for the applicant to engage a solicitor. Court staff will help the applicant and will forward the application to the relevant authority. The authority will check that the application is in order and send it to the foreign authority or court for registration and enforcement against the person living there. The application abroad will be enforced according to the laws that prevail in the foreign country. The UK authorities have no power to compel foreign courts or authorities to enforce maintenance orders, or to set a timescale for enforcement, as the system is based on mutual agreement.

The one thing you have to keep asking yourself when you are going through divorce is do I still have the energy to fight? The 'fight' may be non-physical, non-verbal and mainly require you to just keep going with the processes that are standard, but it does require fight. With this new development, which again required a lot of time and energy, I felt my fight was going to be never-ending.

Suggestions

If you are arranging times for your ex-partner to see your children, agree that both sides will keep to the arrangements, regardless of changing circumstances. Not telling your children until just before they are going to see their other parent may prevent heartache if the meeting does have to be cancelled at the last moment.

Alongside getting support in your community, it's important to give yourself support from within. A good way to start is beginning an inner dialogue, and using mantras. This will build your self-esteem. Whether you are running a marathon, or going through divorce, the words you speak to yourself have huge impact. Tell yourself: everything will work out, I am strong, I am worthy, and I am a great mum. When I am on a tough run I say, over and over 'I can keep going'. This is also something I would say to myself everyday, upon waking, during my separation.

- During tough times give your children space to express themselves, or not express themselves. Don't seek reassurance from them about your own insecurities. Expect anger that may bubble over into physical aggression. When this happens, instantly explain to them that their behaviour is not appropriate, reassuring them that there are other ways to express their emotions. Always try to end difficult situations by explaining to your children that their feelings are natural, but they must find a way to express them in a way that doesn't hurt other people.
- Not all children are aggressive. Some become very compliant and extra-easy to live with, but the hurt goes inwards and makes them ill. Others lose their way at school or find it impossible to make friends or they become silent and withdrawn. Some hurt and harm themselves, some overeat or stop eating altogether. Some just want to die in order to end the pain of loss and the knowledge that they are in the way at a time of great difficulty.
- If you are really worried about your child's behaviour visit your GP and seek advice.
- If your ex-partner now lives abroad, contact the Reciprocal Enforcement of Maintenance Order (REMO) Unit to gain help in registering and enforcing child maintenance orders internationally:

  www.gov.uk/remo-unit-helpline or
  remo@offsol.gsi.gov.uk
  Telephone: 020 3681 2757
  From outside the UK: +44 (0)20 3681 2757

- If a relative decides that now you are alone and vulnerable, this is a great time to make sexual advances to you or even assault you, get help – even from the police if necessary.

- Some of you may not have considered what will happen when you are older, and you may think that whatever pension your husband has paid into will enable you to have a pension that you can live on. This is highly unlikely. As long as you don't remarry or live with someone else as a couple, you will be entitled to a state pension on the back of the payments your ex has made – assuming he worked throughout his life and paid all his National Insurance payments. Sadly the state pension is now so small that it won't do much to keep you in your old age, but it's better than nothing.

- Pension Credits may top up a less than full pension, but they are hard to get and easy to lose if the Department of Work and Pensions suddenly decides not to continue paying this.

- If your ex-husband has paid into a private pension scheme, this won't automatically do anything for you, but your solicitor may be able to fight for some share to come your way. Your best bet is to work, pay your full National Insurance and ensure that you get everything to which you are entitled when you retire. If you can afford to pay into a private scheme, it might be worth doing so, and don't be tempted to turn this into cash if you suddenly find yourself in need of money. If you can't continue paying into the pension plan, ask if it can be halted until you can afford to go back to making payments once again.

Step Five to a New You

How is your running going? Are you starting to think about yourself as a 'real' runner? With your race drawing ever closer, you could be forgiven for starting to feel a few pre-event butterflies. Don't worry; you've got plenty of training miles in the bank. What you need to do now is to focus on getting race-ready. An effective training programme is all about variety. It's a common beginner's mistake to think that getting better at running is about running more. It's not – it's about running smarter. Try to include a longer run, a session with hills or short efforts and one steady run. If you struggle to find time, jog alongside your children on the school run and then run home. Whatever you manage to do is a positive step forward in reaching your goal(s).

If this feels too challenging and your training isn't going to plan, it's time to adjust your goals. If competing isn't for you, how about hooking up with like-minded friends every week to make your fitness time more sociable. You could even consider setting up your own RunTogether group. You don't need any qualifications, just the desire to share the love!

Spend five minutes writing down three mantras that reinforce the positive progress you've made in reaching this stage of your 'recovery'. Start each one with the words 'I am ...' Make sure you repeat these to yourself as you go to sleep at night. Every time you look in the mirror say to yourself: 'I am grateful for being me.'

....

....

....

CHAPTER SIX

*'There is a place called happiness, it is just an arm's length
away from your fears and a few steps beyond your
misgivings. To get there sometimes you need to take the
path of courage down to the street of never-give-up until
you reach the field of dreams.'*
DODINSKY

It wasn't until January 2014 that my reciprocal
arrangement was fully set up and I received
maintenance from my ex-husband – a long four years
since separation!

What helped me to keep going during such a long-
drawn out experience? Even though running had a
big part to play in keeping my body in shape during
these tough years I turned to an emotional wellness
coach to help me knock my emotions into shape. By
unlocking the power of my mind I was able to keep
fighting and facing the new challenges that arose
throughout my experience.

I tried to recover my health and lift my heart out of
my feet after my dad died. Yet only six weeks after
returning to running – and a five kilometre personal
best bagged along the short road down which I had
come – I collapsed at the end of a local five-mile race.

I didn't need anyone to tell me it was all too much.
Motherhood, career, housekeeping, family life, running -
all had created both physical and psychological
overload. I didn't just break down; I found there were no

longer any spare parts left with which to fix or re-boot my system. My main symptom was extreme fatigue. This was accompanied by sleep problems, weight loss (despite an increased appetite) and sometimes feeling I was unable to cope with the everyday. I was open to any and all suggestions in my desperation to get to marathon training in honour of my dad.

I met with Janet Smith, who was qualified in spectrum emotional coaching, counselling, NLP (neuro-linguistic programming) and hypnotherapy. This means Janet helps people explore why they act and react in certain situations, allowing them to stay calmer when challenged and overcome the things that stop them.

When I first talked to Janet she explained further: 'By combining the various therapies, including spectrum emotional coaching, I can get to the root cause of the issue quickly, leaving the person feeling lighter and inspired to take the next steps.'

After discussion, we decided my best option was a 'change day'. This involved six hours (with breaks) of work, where, through gentle relaxation I was able to identify the root causes of the issues that were holding me back and let go of the anger, fear and guilt that had (unknown to me) been dictating my life for so many years.

The work we did was incredibly tough and it involved me taking myself back to the first memories that I associated with the negative emotions. The beauty of spectrum therapy is that it is content free. You do not have to revisit traumatic or problem areas of your life, which is especially important for domestic violence, rape, traumatic births and so on. Colours are associated with each memory, and once we had identified the root of the emotion, Janet helped me to let go of it. After six hours I was shattered.

However, though still exhausted the next day, my feelings and my mind started to settle and I felt clearer about myself. I instantly noticed that I had more patience and tolerance with my children's demands, rather than feeling they were one step too far at the end of another long day.

I also felt secure within. It's hard to explain what the changes meant, except perhaps for a sense of grace. Fun also crept back in to my life. Even though I had realised I was in deep waters, I had no idea what it was that I was carrying around slung over my shoulder – how deep and far back the rejection/fear/pain/guilt went.

During the session, and each wave of clearing a negative emotion, I had no idea what to expect. Where Janet took me, through hypnosis, to find the root cause of the emotion was a complete surprise. Mostly it involved going back to my early childhood days and talking about how I felt rejected by both parents, as well as being fearful of the future. Even though I felt fully aware of what Janet was saying and how it all linked together inside, by the next day I couldn't really recall exactly where it was my mind had travelled to. I retain glimpses of the issues that she dealt with, but the roots that she took me back to are shrouded in vague mists of memory.

Two weeks later I started to feel the way I did before I had burnt-out. I felt like cooking tea and taking the girls out – something that I had struggled with all that summer. I got back on my treadmill, and while it was tiring, it wasn't impossible. Most importantly I began to feel less burdened.

By October I was ready to return to running, and with the gentle encouragement of my running buddy, Penny, we slowly ran a little further, with many giggles along the way. I committed to running the Reggae Half Marathon at the beginning of December with David, and I did it, finishing fifth female vet (veteran) as an extra bonus during one of the craziest but most exciting weekends of my life. December saw me return to my beloved, tough, soul-destroying but endorphin-mad cross-country running.

Using emotional wellness therapy wasn't just a once off for me, as I have returned to Janet regarding other issues, including dealing with feelings related to my ex-husband and issues surrounding my running. For me it was a turning point in my 'recovery' from divorce, and it is a long-term commitment that I have made to myself to face my fears. If I feel overwhelmed or realise that I am holding myself back regarding certain issues I book in to speak to Janet, who, during a 60 or 90-minute session, can help me clear away any negative emotions that may have returned. I also find it very spiritual, because when I explore the roots of all the emotions that we have worked on, they all lead back to the quest for inner peace. One of the most powerful sessions that I had, helped me to realise that my ex-husband is only trying to find his own inner peace through his journey, and I learned to respect that in this way we are no different.

With help from this therapy I've been able to let go of the negative emotions attached to my separation and divorce. I stood on the start-line of Edinburgh Marathon in May 2014. The final month of training didn't go to plan, as marathons often don't, and it was such an emotional few weeks for me, while I slowly came to terms with my dad's death the year before.

I hadn't done the long runs I needed due to a long-standing hip injury, but David helped me believe I could at least give the race a try. I finished it by walking the last seven miles. At the end I cried my eyes out as I limped back to the park-and-ride station, hanging on to David. Everything flooded out, a river of unconscious feelings escaping through every pore of my body. I wanted to run a marathon in memory of my dad. I've still got to do this, as I didn't actually run all of Edinburgh, but I did finish the race. I just have a new challenge to complete, and until I run through a whole race I won't feel I've truly said goodbye to my dad.

However hard the race was, I still finished. I survived; despite a broken body, I maintained enough control to see the experience through to the end. Once the tears finally stopped coming I felt happy; despite having to walk and losing control of my left hip I had carried on. Despite wobbling along for miles I had the strength to finish. Looking back I don't know how I carried on when my hip had seized but I did. I just put one foot in front of the other.

Deep within me I began to feel that it was time for life to move on. David, the girls and I thrived as a family, despite our complicated lives. His children live in Yorkshire, so he is often away visiting them and my girls rarely see their dad. My inner strength had returned. As this gradually happens for you, and you feel that you are in more control of your life, you may also consider a new relationship, or maybe you have already found a new partner and are beginning this new phase of life post-separation.

If your separation and divorce are complicated, the kindest thing you can do for yourself is work your way through the experience you are in before embarking on a new relationship. It's very hard to welcome a new partner into your life, and focus on your new relationship, when you are still trying to end another long-term relationship. However, life doesn't often work in such a sensible manner!

Our work, and love of running, brought David and me together, and even though I had been separated for over a year when we met, I had no idea that it would take another three before I could move on from sorting out my divorce. So the first few years of our relationship were often fraught with emotional issues and each year seemed to become more and more complicated. However, David stood by the girls and me until we finally made it to the end of our divorce road. At times I was so troubled by the struggle I withdrew deep inside myself and would barely talk to him. Yet he didn't give up on me, and, when grief and confusion overwhelmed me, he took over the job of looking after the girls. When my self-esteem was at rock bottom he never stopped believing in me, or us – both as a couple, and a family.

Blended families like ours can be complicated and hard to manage, and it can seem impossible at times to please everyone in your life. We have five children between us, so holidays are not very relaxing! Whoever you are, and whatever your situation, when you come to the end of your divorce road, you will realise how much stronger the experience has made you. Everything else that is meant to be will flow from this position of strength.

If someone had told me on that bleak winter's day in February 2010 that I would survive the experience that was ahead of me, that I would be strong enough to face endless challenges and be able to support my children and provide them with a stable, loving, understanding family life that focused on promoting their self-esteem and give them the best chances I wouldn't have believed them. If someone had whispered in my ear, saying that life would conspire to give me the opportunity to meet a new partner who would be my soul mate, and that there would be no need for so much anxiety, stress and worry, I would have found it impossible to believe. You will also survive, become stronger, and eventually find love.

When I first considered divorce I was petrified. I wavered over my decision. I was fearful of the future. What I imagined the divorce process to be didn't happen and what I dreaded the most came true. My girls have grown up with little contact with their dad. However, at no stage over the last seven years have I regretted my decision. Even if I had known what was ahead in February 2010, I still wouldn't have stayed in our marriage. I couldn't spend the rest of my life with someone I didn't love. My great regret is that we couldn't sort out our separation and divorce more amicably, and that the girls have seen so little of their dad for so many years of their lives. However, their love for him never diminishes, and as they grow older I know they will re-build their relationship with their dad, just as I did with mine when I hit a crucial stage in my life.

The girls also have a step-dad who is involved in their day-to-day life, and who nags them to tidy up after themselves, referees their fights, ferries them around and reassures them that they are loved at the end of each day.

After many ups and downs, my running is slowly returning to the standard at which I was pre-divorce, and recently I was in the bronze-medal team at the England 10-mile championships. I'm training for London Marathon, and yes, I'm hoping for a personal best! Moving into the Vet45 (veteran over 45 years of age) category is not going to slow me down!

Today my overwhelming sense is of peace, and the knowledge that I CAN cope, with whatever is going to happen. You too will survive this experience, you will provide your children with as much love and support you can, and there's a good chance you will go on to find new love, that fits so much better because it is will have developed from a place of peace, happiness and strength.

Romance will be knocking on your door before you know it, I am sure! Whether you meet someone or dabble with online dating (and with sites that offer compatible matching, such as eHarmony, you'll probably meet someone before you think) let your destiny take you where you need to go. Think positive thoughts about the relationship you desire and it will come to you. And be excited at the journey! This is YOUR life!

Suggestions

If you are struggling to get into some of the new challenges you have set yourself, try to be really honest with yourself. What are your thoughts around fitness? Were your parents active? What about your siblings? This will help you become aware of what views may have become imprinted in your mind as you were growing up, and the journey you are now travelling through. By unpicking what's imprinted, you can heal emotional issues and decide what your success will give to you.

Be open to success: Think: 'What would I feel like if I completed my goal?'

'Whatever your fitness journey is, cultivate kindness towards your body,' says Janet Smith.

This allows you to understand exactly what it is going to take for your body to get you to your destination. Whether you're training for a 5K, 10K, half-marathon or some other race distance, there's a good chance that if you're not emotionally well in addition to being physically fit, you may not reach your target or goal. We all create beliefs around our own experiences, and sometimes our parents – who label us as clever, sporty, arty or useless – can reinforce this. Therefore, it's important to be open to success.

Love your physical form: Listen to your body with kindness when an issue comes up. If you get pain or injury, it's likely you've been pushing your body too much for a while. If you look back can you realise the signs it was sending you?

Stay positive: Ignoring your inner critic is vital to this!

'If you can hear a voice in your head criticising yourself or being negative, ask yourself whose voice is it?' says Janet Smith. 'Your own? Your parents'? You will need to make peace with this voice and banish negative self-talk!'

If you can recognise the voice, you can change it to that of someone who motivates you - a celebrity, an athlete, even your personal trainer. What would they say to you? If you are running through loss, imagine what the person you have lost would say to you when your running gets tough. Use their voice to bring a positive attitude to your running.

Be present: Janet believes it is important to be aware of what is happening around you on your run.

She suggests that you, 'Look up from the ground and notice the sky and the light. Taking in the bigger picture can be liberating as you are connecting with your surroundings and nature. Practise mindfulness, even if for only a few minutes at a time during your warm up or warm down.'

Belong: Did you realise that, even if you run alone, you are still a member of a universal club along with millions of other like-minded people?

'Know that as a runner you are never alone,' says Janet.

Many of us don't live close to our families, but belonging to a running community can help to fill this void and help you feel less isolated.

Step Six to a New You
Race day has finally arrived and it's time to put your weeks and months of training into action. Getting to this stage is as big an achievement as running the race itself. As you stand on the start-line, remember why you're here and the journey you've taken to get to this point. You may find that you're extremely emotional – this is normal. When you reach the finish it's almost as if you have finally proved to yourself that you can succeed in your life and that you are strong. Whatever stage your divorce is at, this can help you focus on positive emotions and outcomes. No matter what emotions you are feeling, don't get dragged into going off too fast when the gun sounds. Adrenalin has a lot to

answer for! The temptation to keep pace with people around you can lead you to forget about your pre-race plan: don't! Stick to your well-drilled pacing strategy, and if it's your first race, err on the side of caution. It's better to finish feeling strong and with the knowledge that you could have given more, than to cross the line as an emotional and physical wreck. With your first race now in the bag, it's time to start thinking about new goals, because your running goals can become a metaphor for those in your life. Now's the time to identify and plan some running and fitness goals for the short-term, medium-term and long-term. Whatever comes next is up to you – remember, your imagination can take you anywhere.

- If this feels too challenging there are many events that you can enter that require you to walk or cycle at your own pace, rather than run. Moon Walks, and Ride the Night (www.ridethenight.co.uk) give all women, regardless of age or fitness the opportunity to take part in non-competitive, fun events, and to raise money for others at the same time.

Spend five minutes writing down three different goals you want to achieve; a personal goal, a health goal and a life goal.

....

....

....

CONCLUSION

'When something bad happens you have three choices. You can either let it define you, let it destroy you or you can let it strengthen you.'
UNKNOWN.

So there are your choices. You can find the courage to let your separation and divorce make you a stronger person. Apart from losing a loved one, divorce is probably the hardest life experience you will encounter – and yet, you can survive it. When you are old, and you look back at the challenges that you are currently going through, the likelihood is you probably won't remember all of them. Hopefully, as life moves onward, they won't matter as much as they do now.

We all create our own realities, and we all attract into our lives energy that is similar to our own thoughts and the feelings that we give out. Failure to let go of our anger - the burning coal that only hurts the person who holds it – brings negativity into our lives.

Think about what imprint you want to leave on this life. Energy that resonates with anger, or using your life force to overcome difficult obstacles by taking a different path, one of forgiveness, love and compassion, not just for those who may have hurt or wronged you, but for yourself. You have all the answers you need in your own hands. There's a good chance you are exactly where you need to be in your life, although you may need time to realise this.

Being able to recognise the emotions linked to grief takes courage, especially if they are linked to deeper, suppressed feelings. Facing your fears and feelings of anger, may help you to be able to express them in a healthy way, rather than through spite or revenge.

Focusing positively on bringing what you need into your life can yield great rewards leading to inner peace, which is the ultimate happiness. Those times when we wake up or get ready for bed are powerful moments in our day, and times when we can bring positive images, thoughts, mantras and emotions into focus.

Relationships, family, home and career... you can refocus the lens on all of these at this time, seeing how you want them to develop. You have the power within you to change your life every day. It's time to look at who you really are and appreciate the person you have become.

Leave behind the negative thoughts and people who are toxic. Set yourself new goals, whether they are weekly, monthly or yearly, social, health or career. Feel that you are in control, but also expect some wobbles. This is life!

The challenges will get easier, and as you find your feet financially and re-establish a sense of self, feelings of calm and dignity will return. Every time you look in the mirror, remind yourself of three simple thoughts: 'I am amazing. I am strong. I am brave.' Enjoy your life as it unfolds with love and eagerness, and allow all you need to flow into your life now. And maybe running, or some other form of exercise, will help you get your twenty-first century lifestyle back in sync with your stone-age body. You may even grow to like your 200,000-year-old self.

With the benefit of all this life experience you will sail into your future. Having known uncertainty you can ensure that your happiness and that of your family is certain. Having known sadness, you can make sure your future focuses on happiness, contentment and peace. You can heal yourself, and from your position of strength you can build the rest of your life on love. Just put one foot in front of the other.

There's also a good chance you will, if you allow yourself, eventually be able to remember the love upon which your ex-partner and you first built your relationship on. As your emotional wounds heal, your ultimate aim is to be able to move forwards in life and focus on the fact that you both chose each other to be the parent of your children. This is better than dwelling on the pain you have suffered, as you both struggled to walk down an unknown path, as this will help you unite when your children, facing their own fears, call upon you both for help.

* * *

Work For You to Engage In
Tap into your creativity.
In order to succeed at your chosen goal, Janet Smith suggests you:
Allow yourself five minutes when you won't be interrupted and where it's peaceful and quiet and use meditation to bring your mind into the present. Now imagine yourself waking up on the day after you have achieved your goal.

- What are you feeling?
- What do you see?
- What are you saying to yourself?
- What does your success mean to you?

You may feel pride that you have left your past behind and shown your children you can be fit throughout your life. Once you achieve your goal, you can aim for a bigger one.

Now ask these same questions of the people who are important to you:

- Do you feel loved from the support they have given you?
- Perhaps you have inspired a partner or child who is trying to lose weight and start an exercise programme?
- What about the wider community?
- Can you see that you have shown other women that they can also achieve their goals?
- Can you hear positive stories about your achievement?
- Have you demonstrated that age doesn't have to be a barrier to running?

Write the answers down as you think of them.

Be Present When You Run

If you are used to chatting with a friend when you run, try spending the last five minutes of your session doing the opposite – being quiet, each in your own space. After the run, ask each other what you noticed, for example, the sunlight bouncing off a gate.

- If you are a solitary runner who prefers to be quiet while you run, challenge yourself to notice your environment. Don't just do this in your head; try and connect with your surroundings using your senses. What can you hear, smell and see?
- If you are usually in sync with your environment, take this a step further and practise gratitude for what you see and feel… for your heart pumping, your muscles contracting in your legs or your lungs breathing. Check in with your body and ask yourself if you can feel your energy?

APPENDIX

Here is my 10-Week Beginners' Training Plan:

	Day 1	Day 2	Day 3	Day 4	Day 5	Day 6	Day 7
Week 1	Walk 5mins Run 5mins Walk 5mins	Walk 20mins	Rest	Walk 7mins Run 7mins Walk 7mins	Single leg Squats 30-secs plank	Run 10mins	Walk 30mins
Week 2	Rest	Walk 25mins	Rest	Run 10mins Walk 5mins Run 10mins	Stretching Calf raises	Rest	Walk/Run 40mins
Week 3	Rest	Run 12mins Walk 5mins Run 12mins	Swim or bike	Run 15mins	Rest	Run 15mins Walk 10mins Run 10mins Walk 5mins Run 3mins	Rest
Week 4	Walk 25mins	Swim or bike	Rest	Run 12mins Walk 5mins Run 10mins Walk 5mins Run 6mins	Rest	Run 25mins	Stretching
Week 5	Run 25mins	Rest	Swim or bike	Run 10mins Walk 3mins Run 10mins Walk 3mins Run 10mins	Rest	Run 25mins	60secs plank Single leg squats Stretching

	Day 1	Day 2	Day 3	Day 4	Day 5	Day 6	Day 7
Week 6	Hills (5 x 45 secs)	Rest	Run 20mins	Swim	Rest	Run 5mins easy Run 2mins faster Repeat x 5	Rest
Week 7	Rest	Hills 25mins: Run up, Jog down recovery	Rest	Run 25mins	Rest	Run 5mins Run 10mins Faster x 2	Stretching
Week 8	30mins hill repeats	Rest	Swim or bike	Run 20 – 30mins easy	Rest	Run 45mins	Rest
Week 9	Bike or swim	Hills 30mins	Rest	Run 4 x 5mins Increasing pace	Rest	Run 30mins easy	Rest
Week 10	Swim or bike	Speed runs 8 x 1mins	Rest	Run 20mins easy	Rest	Rest	10Km RACE

Useful Books

The Story of the Human Body
    by Daniel Lieberman
Wishes Fulfilled
    by Wayne Dyer
Ruling your world: Ancient strategies for modern life
    by Sakyong Miphram
Getting into the Vortex
    by Ester and Jerry Hicks
The Secret, The Magic, The Power
    by Rhonda Byrne
The Power of Now
    by Eckhart Tolle
Learning to Love Yourself by Gay Hendricks
Men are from Mars and Women are from Venus
    by John Gray
The Miracle Morning
    by Hal Elrod
How to save an hour everyday
    by Michael Heppell
Steve Biddulph's Raising Girls
    by Steve Biddulph
Raising Boys
    by Steve Biddulph
Putting children first: A handbook for separated parents
    by Karen Woodall
Was it the chocolate pudding?
    by Sandra Levins
It's not your fault Koko bear
    by Vicki Lansky
Your Pace or Mine?
    by Lisa Jackson

Finding Help
Lynda Panter:
www.healing-hypnotherapy.co.uk, tel: 023 92 436 698
Janet Smith:
www.emotionalwellnesscoaching.co.uk,
tel: 07966 552439

For your local spectrum therapist:
www.spectrumhealthandwellbeing.com

INDEX

Citizen's Advice Centre 28
CMS 64
Colours 82
complementary therapies 66
counselling 82
CSA 63

D
Dalglish, Lisa 61, 70
David 84, 85
Department of Work and Pensions 79
Dyer, Wayne 18, 33
dyslexia 9

E
EBay 66
eHarmony 87
ELSA 61, 65
Emotional Literacy Support Assistant 61, 65
emotional wellness therapy 84
Endorphins 66
exercise 66

F
FaceTime 70
fairy godmother 61
Family therapy 72
financial plan 38
Find a Solicitor 37
Fit Ball 19

G
Getting into the Vortex 37
gingerbread 38
group cycling 19

H
Hicks, Jerry 37